Contemporary MOOD LAMPS

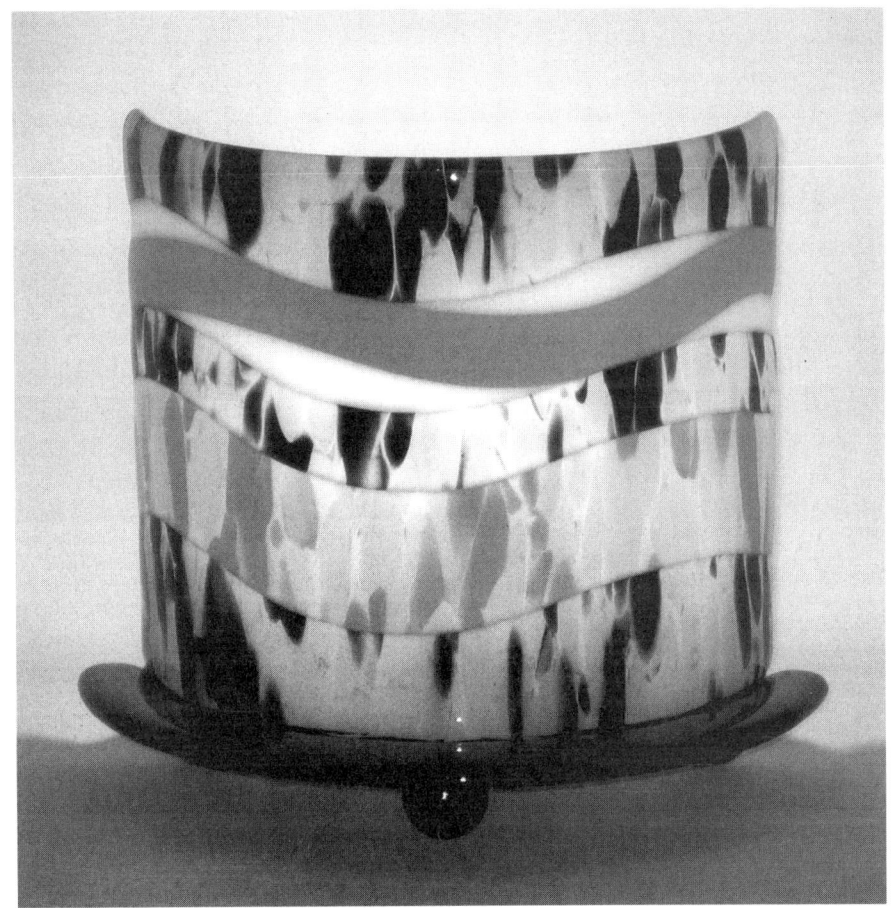

Martin Gill

CKE Publications
Olympia, WA

From the Author...

Warm glass is quite new to me, having been a potter for some thirty years. I was visiting fellow artist Christine Stewart at her glass studio on the east coast of Australia where I discovered the beauty and diversity of art glass. It was while holding different pieces of glass up to the light I came up with the idea of transforming this beautiful glass into a series of Mood Lamps. That was in mid 2006 and since then with lots of experimenting and converting a pottery kiln into a glass kiln, I was able to come up with some contemporary designs which I retail throughout Australia. I am more than happy to share my techniques and designs with you so that you too can create your own exciting Mood Lamps.

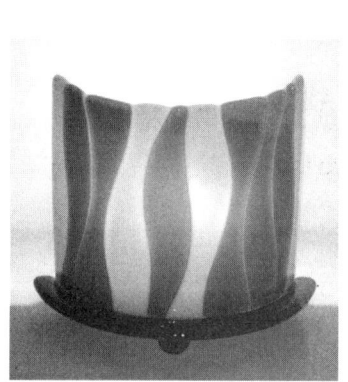 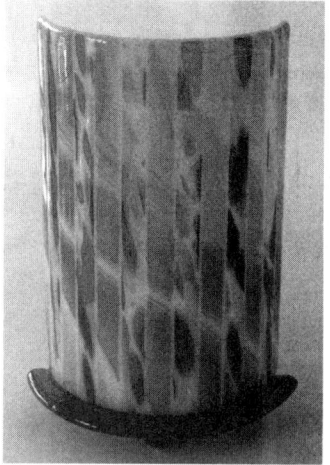 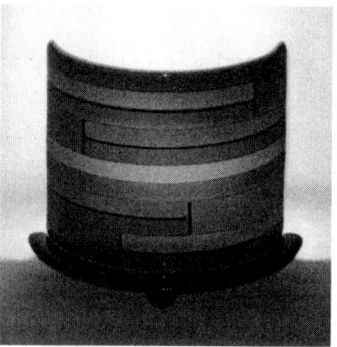

The lamps can also be used as sconces!
Simply eliminate the base and add
a sconce kit available at art glass supply stores.

Every effort has been made to ensure that all information in this book is accurate. However, due to differing conditions, tools, and individual skills, the publisher and author cannot be responsible for any injuries, losses, or other damages that may result from the use of the information in this book.

Book Production: Laura Tayne
Printed in the U.S.A. by: Consolidated Press, Seattle, WA

ISBN 978-1-932327-27-4

Copyright © Martin Gill, 2007. Covers patterns, illustrations, photographs and text used in this publication.

All Rights Reserved. No part of this publication may be reproduced, stored or transmitted in any form or by any means, electronic, mechanical, recording or otherwise, without the prior permission of the copyright owner, with the exception of reproduction of the patterns for personal use only.
Notice to Copy Centers: Permission is given to enlarge any design in this book to the maximum of four copies per customer.

Distribution
CKE PUBLICATIONS
PO Box 12869
Olympia, WA 98508-2869
USA
Tel : (360) 352-4427 FAX: 360-943-3978
E-mail: ckepublications@comcast.net
Web: www.ckepublications.com

Call CKE at 1-800-428-7402 to ask for a free catalog of our books and patterns, also for information about our pattern enlargement service.

About the Lamps...

Our Mood Lamps are comprised of two main fused glass components - The Lamp Lens and the Lamp Base.

The Mood Lamp Lens

Most of the lenses in this book are made by using white opal fusible glass as the foundation layer. White allows excellent light transmission when illuminated.

The top layer that creates the design for the lamp lens can be cut from either opal or transparent, compatible fusible glass. Spectrum and Uroboros have an exciting range of specialty glasses - Spirit, Opal Art, Fractures and Streamers - which will further enhance the designs. The cut design pieces are placed on top of the white foundation glass and fused together. The end result is a sturdy rectangle of glass that is then slumped over a mold to form the curved shape of the lens.

The Mood Lamp Base

The lamp base consists of two and three layers of glass designed to form a strong, grooved structure that the lens can be adhered to.

Once fused, a hole is drilled into the base to allow the fitting of the electrical wiring. The feet are then adhered into position. These feet are simply made from marbles which have a flat area ground onto them and adhered to the underside of the base. The marble feet elevate the lamp.

Before you start...

The patterns in this book are suitable for the **Delphi Glass Round Wall Sconce Mold #4270 or Future Forms Round Sconce Mold WC 40**. Both of these molds are available in the stained glass industry. It is important to source your mold before you start, so that you are making your lamp lens to match the size of your mold.

As an alternative, bisque fired molds are available from your stained glass supply store, and any that are a half round or half cylinder shape will work in creating your mood lamp. It is important, though, to check the size of the mold you are using to the size of the designs in this book. The patterns are easily re-sized if needed.

It is also possible to use a mold from a ceramic shop. I have had success using a cylinder shape that the supplier cut in half before it was bisque fired which was great as it gave me two half-circle molds. To check the size of your mold you will need to take a measurement around the outside curve of the mold and deduct approximately 1" from this measurement (doing this ensures the lamp lens will not touch the kiln shelf when slumping). Compare this measurement to the width of the lamp lens patterns and adjust if required. Check the height also to make sure it is tall enough to fit the pattern.

Materials

Delphi Glass Round Wall Sconce Mold #4270 or Future Forms Round Sconce Mold WC 40 or suitable alternative

- Glass cutting tools
- Compatible glass
- Sharpie marking pen
- Adhesive sealant
- Two-part Epoxy glue
- 1" diameter marbles for lamp feet
- Glass grinder

- Dust mask
- Kiln
- Thin-fire shelf paper & primer
- Kiln shelf primer
- Safety glasses
- Heat protective gloves
- Card stock

- $1/4$" bit for glass grinder - or drill press with $3/8$" (10mm) hollow core diamond drill bit for electrical fitting hole in base
- Lamp kit including socket, cord & fittings available at your hardware store - or have your lamp professionally wired by an electrician

Detailed instructions for creating the components for your Mood Lamp are found on pages 14 through 21.

Lamp 1 Night Magic

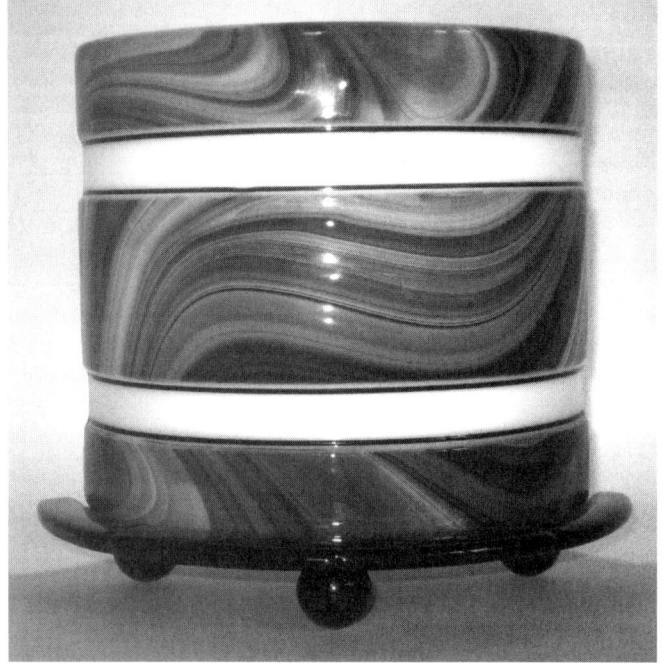

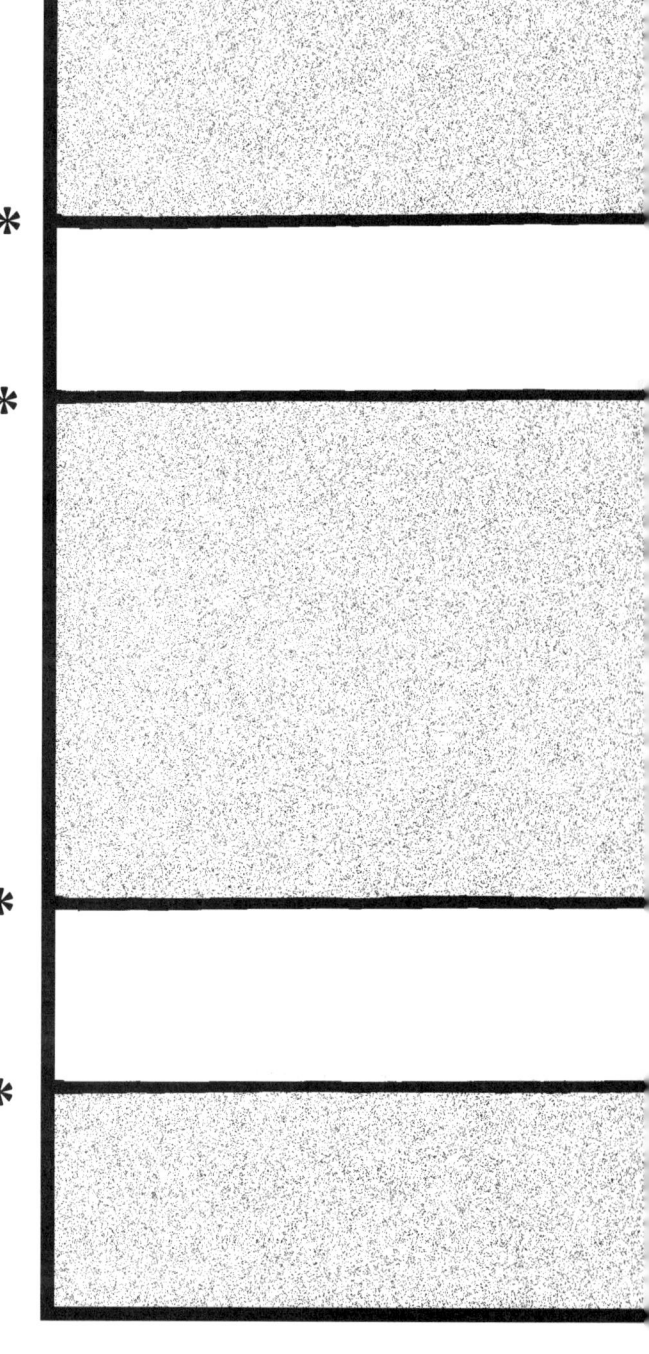

Lamp Base	Spectrum System 96 - Black Opal 1009SF
Lens Base	Spectrum System 96 - White Opal - 200SF
Top Design Layer	Spectrum System 96 - **A** ... Opal Art OA/634-52SF Blackberry Black Stringer

• Cut one lens base the size of pattern above.
• Cut one of each top design layer, marked "**A**". Place these pieces on top of lens base following indications on pattern.
• Position stringer alongside each top layer design piece as marked with an asterisk* on pattern.
• See the detailed instructions on pages 18 and 19 for fabricating the lens and base.

A

(Base Layer)

A

(Base Layer)

A

Use outer perimeter as pattern for the lens base.

✱ = Stringer placement

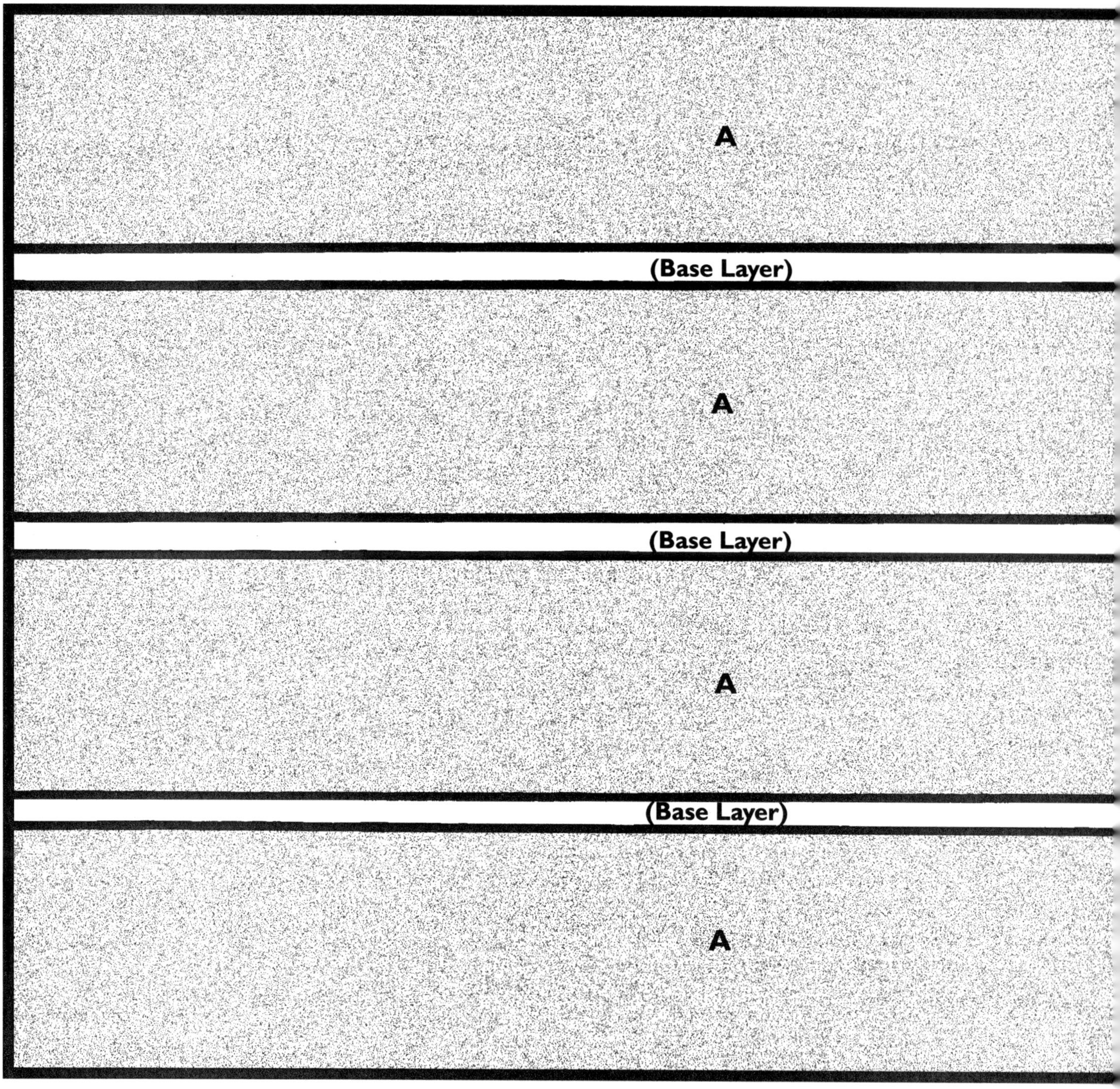

A

(Base Layer)

A

(Base Layer)

A

(Base Layer)

A

Use outer perimeter as pattern for the lens base.

✱ = Stringer placement

Tornado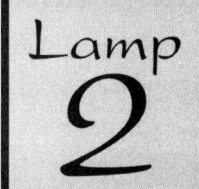

Lamp 2

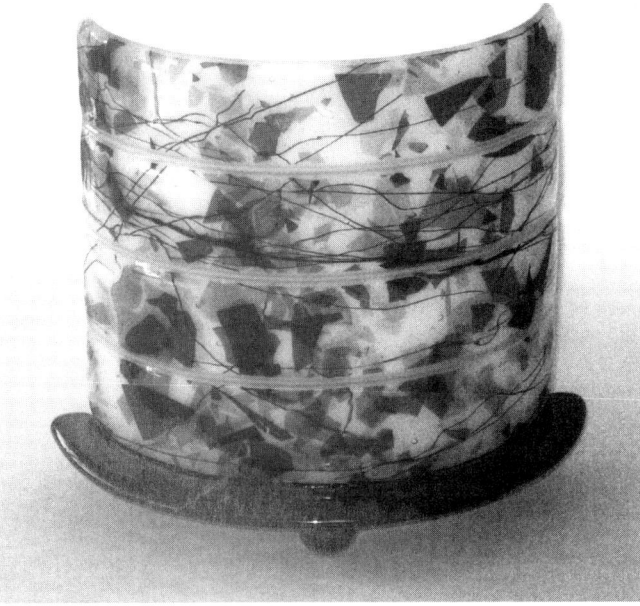

*
*

*
*

*
*

Lamp Base	Spectrum System 96 - Black Opal 1009SF
Lens Base	Spectrum System 96 - White Opal - 200SF
Top Design Layer	Uroboros System 96 - **A**...11-45-96 Clear w/Green & Red Fractures and Streamers

- Cut one lens base the size of pattern above.
- Cut one of each top design layer, marked "**A**". Place these pieces on top of lens base following indications on pattern.
- See the detailed instructions on pages 18 and 19 for fabricating the lens and base.

For an interesting variation, add black stringer or a color of your choice next to each top layer design piece. Positiion stringer at positions marked with an asterisk* on the Layout Diagram.

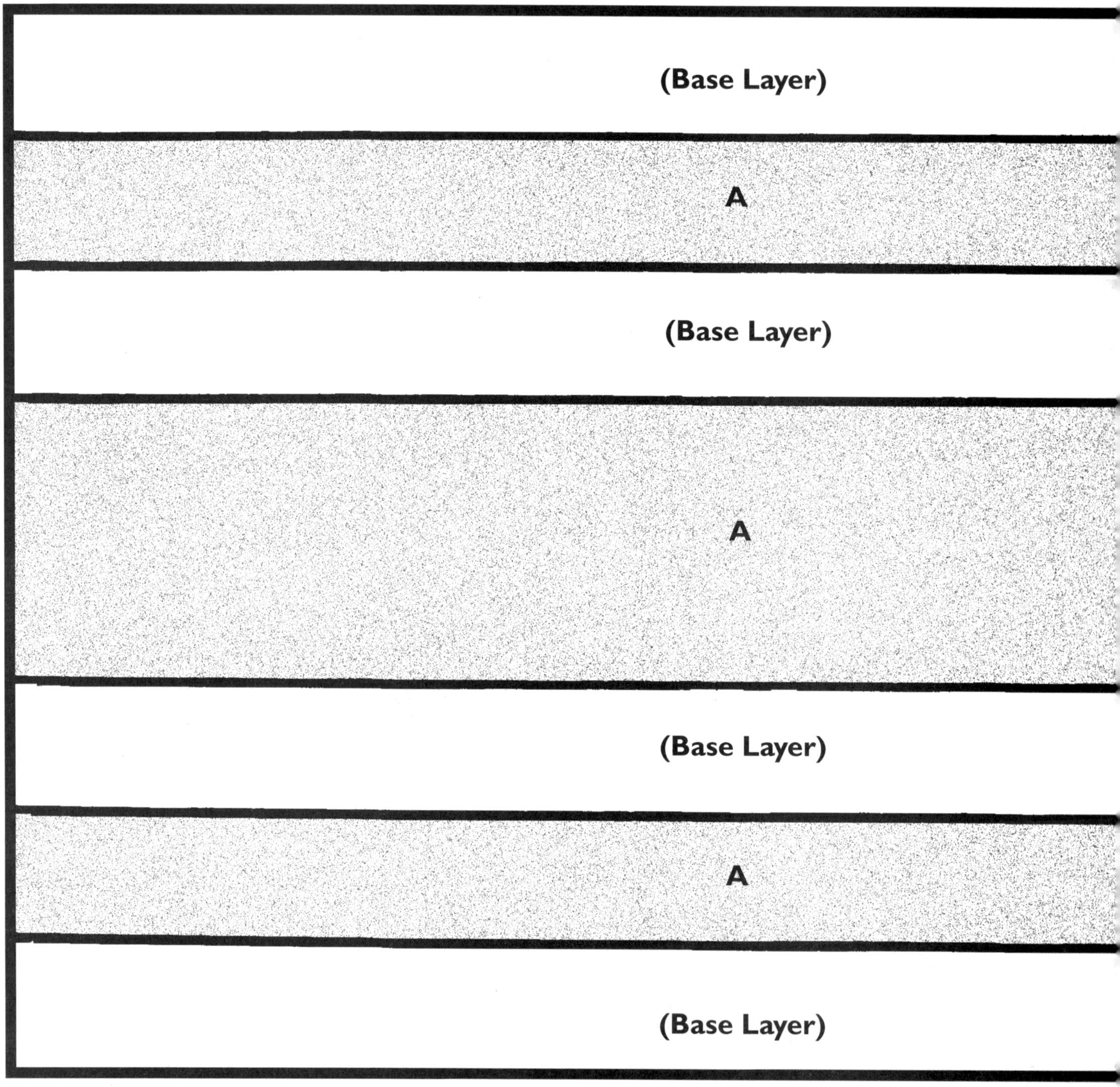

(Base Layer)

A

(Base Layer)

A

(Base Layer)

A

(Base Layer)

Use outer perimeter as pattern for the lens base.

✽ = Stringer placement

Musk Slice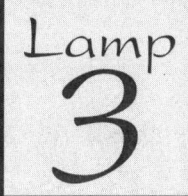

Lamp 3

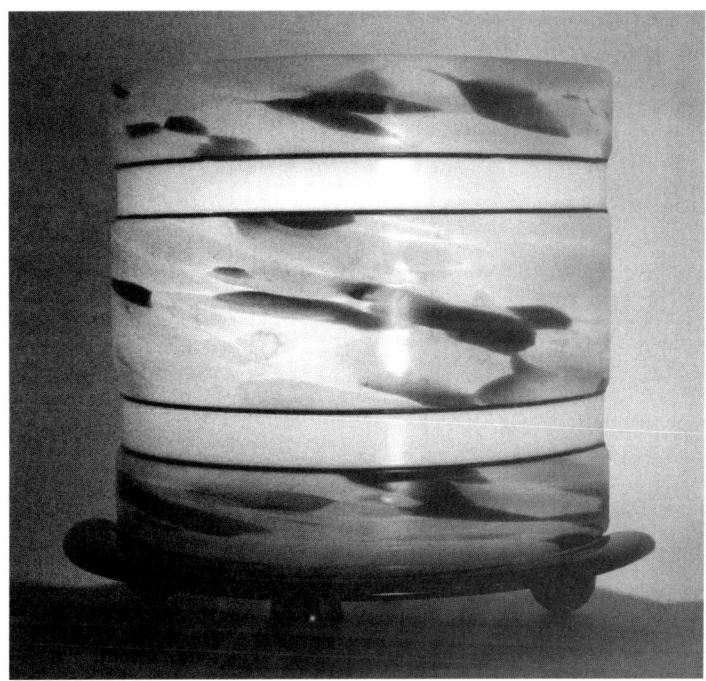

Lamp Base	Spectrum System 96 - Black Opal 1009SF
Lens Base	Spectrum System 96 - White Opal - 200SF
Top Design Layer	Spectrum System 96 - **A** ... Spirit 694-7SF Geneva
	Black Stringer

- Cut one lens base the size of pattern above.
- Cut one of each top design layer, marked "**A**". Place these pieces on top of lens base following indications on pattern.
- Position stringer alongside each top layer design piece as marked with an asterisk* on pattern.
- See the detailed instructions on pages 18 and 19 for fabricating the lens and base.

Lamp 4 Dappled Light

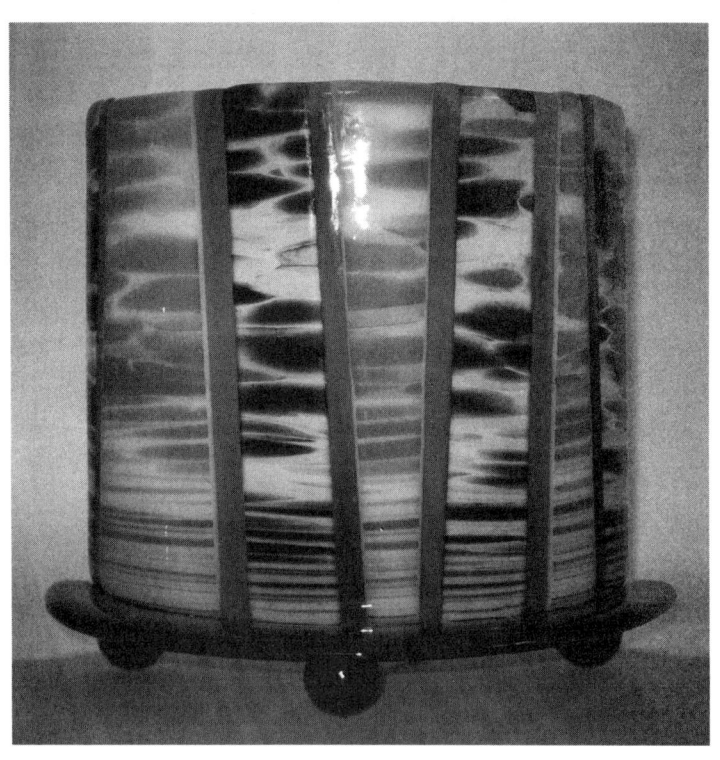

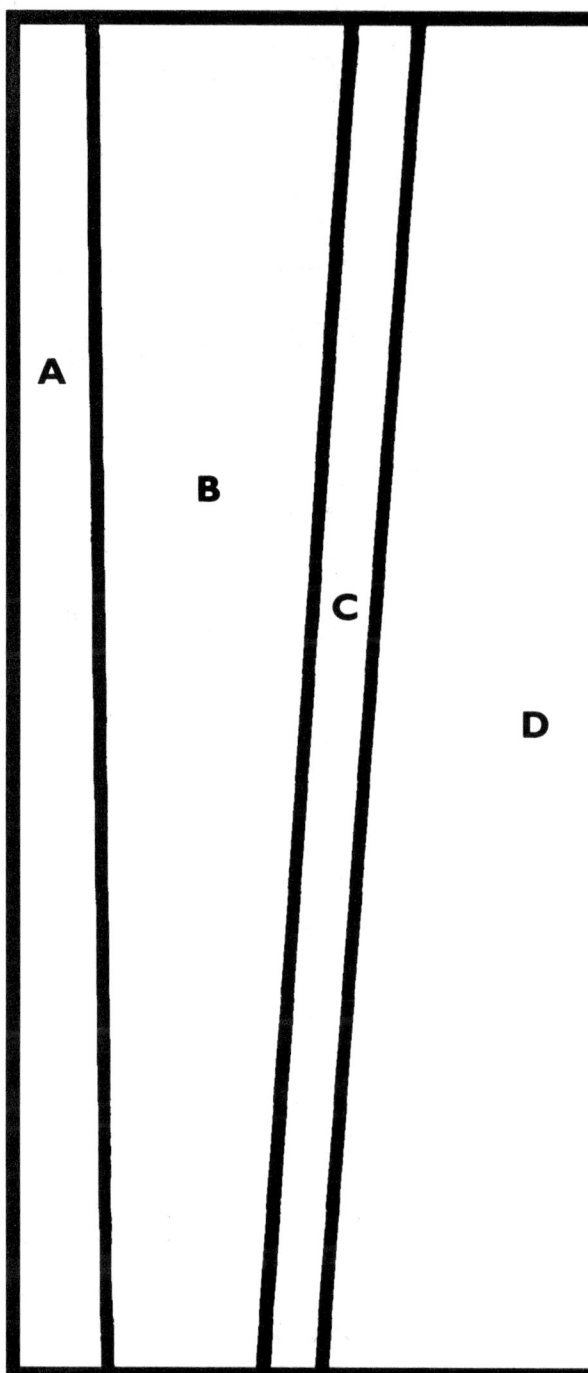

Lamp Base	Spectrum System 96	- Black Opal 1009SF
Lens Base	Spectrum System 96	- White Opal - 200SF
Top Design Layer	Spectrum System 96	- A ... Grape Transparent 543-2SF
		B ... Spirit 4001SF Murano
		C ... Red Transparent 151SF
		D ... Spirit 6115-72SF Sedona
		E ... Teal Transparent 523-2SF

- Cut one lens base the size of pattern above.
- Cut one of each top design layer, marked "**A, B, C, D, E**". Place these pieces on top of lens base following indications on pattern.
- See the detailed instructions on pages 18 and 19 for fabricating the lens and base.

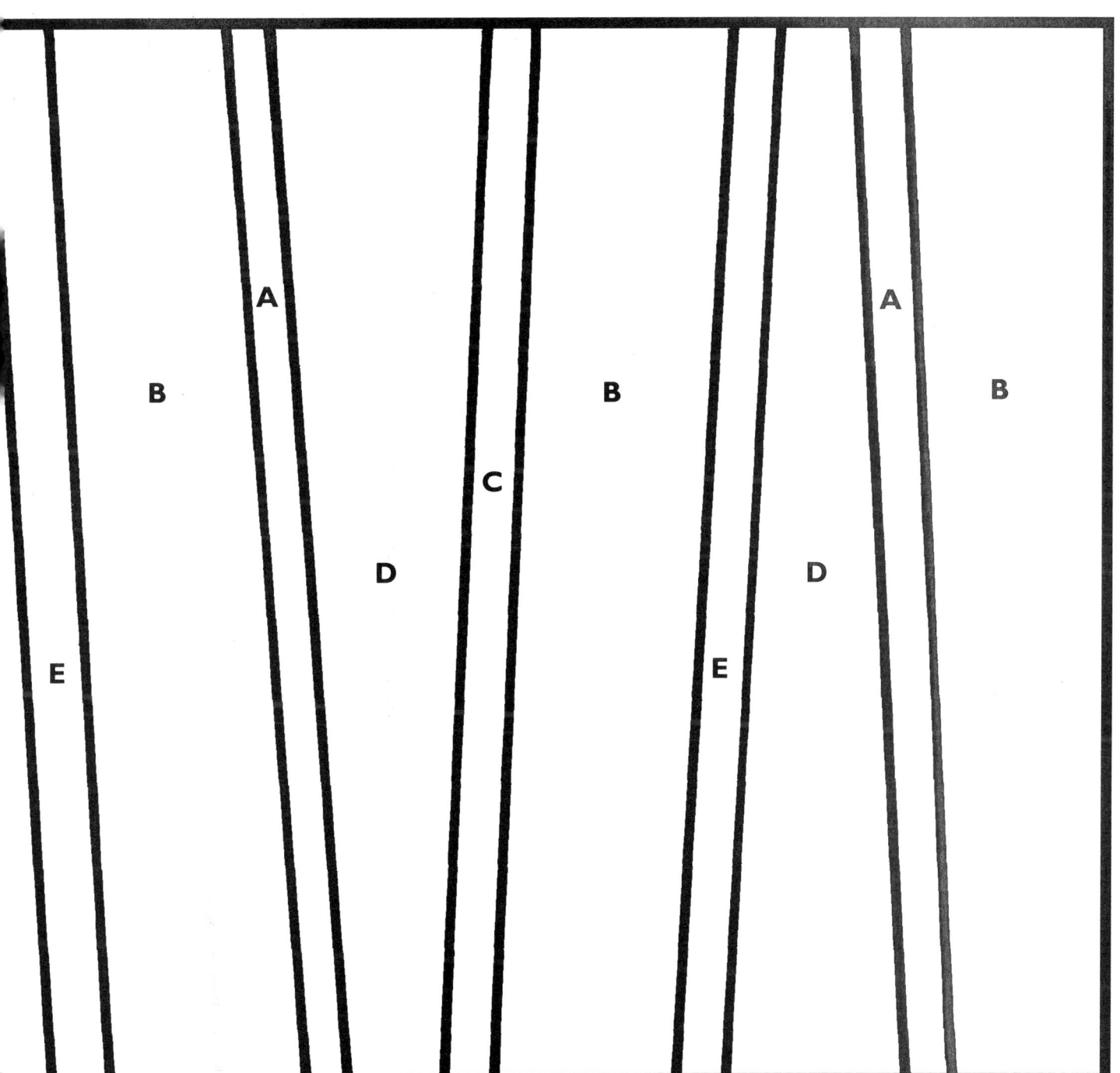

Use outer perimeter as pattern for the lens base.

Lamp 5 Neon Glow

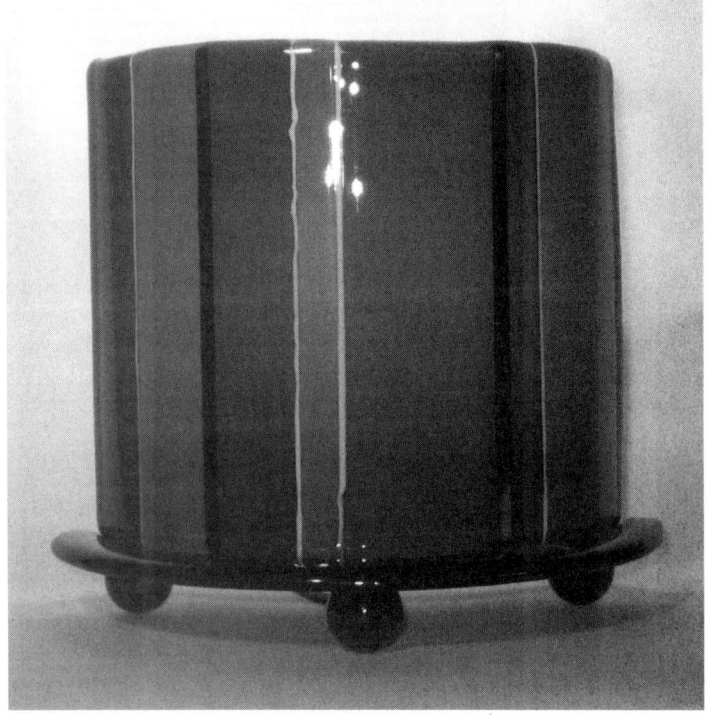

| A | B | C |

Dichroic rainbow noodle on black

*

Lamp Base	Spectrum System 96 -	Black Opal 1009SF
Lens Base	Spectrum System 96 -	White Opal - 200SF
Top Design Layer	Spectrum System 96 -	**A** ... Deep Aqua Transparent 533-3SF
		B ... Moss Green Transparent 526-2SF
		C ... Grape Transparent 543-2SF
		Dichroic rainbow noodle on black

- Cut one lens base the size of pattern above.
- Cut one of each top design layer, marked "**A**, **B** & **C**". Place these pieces on top of lens base following indications on pattern.
- Position dichroic rainbow noodle following the indications on pattern.
- See the detailed instructions on pages 18 and 19 for fabricating the lens and base.

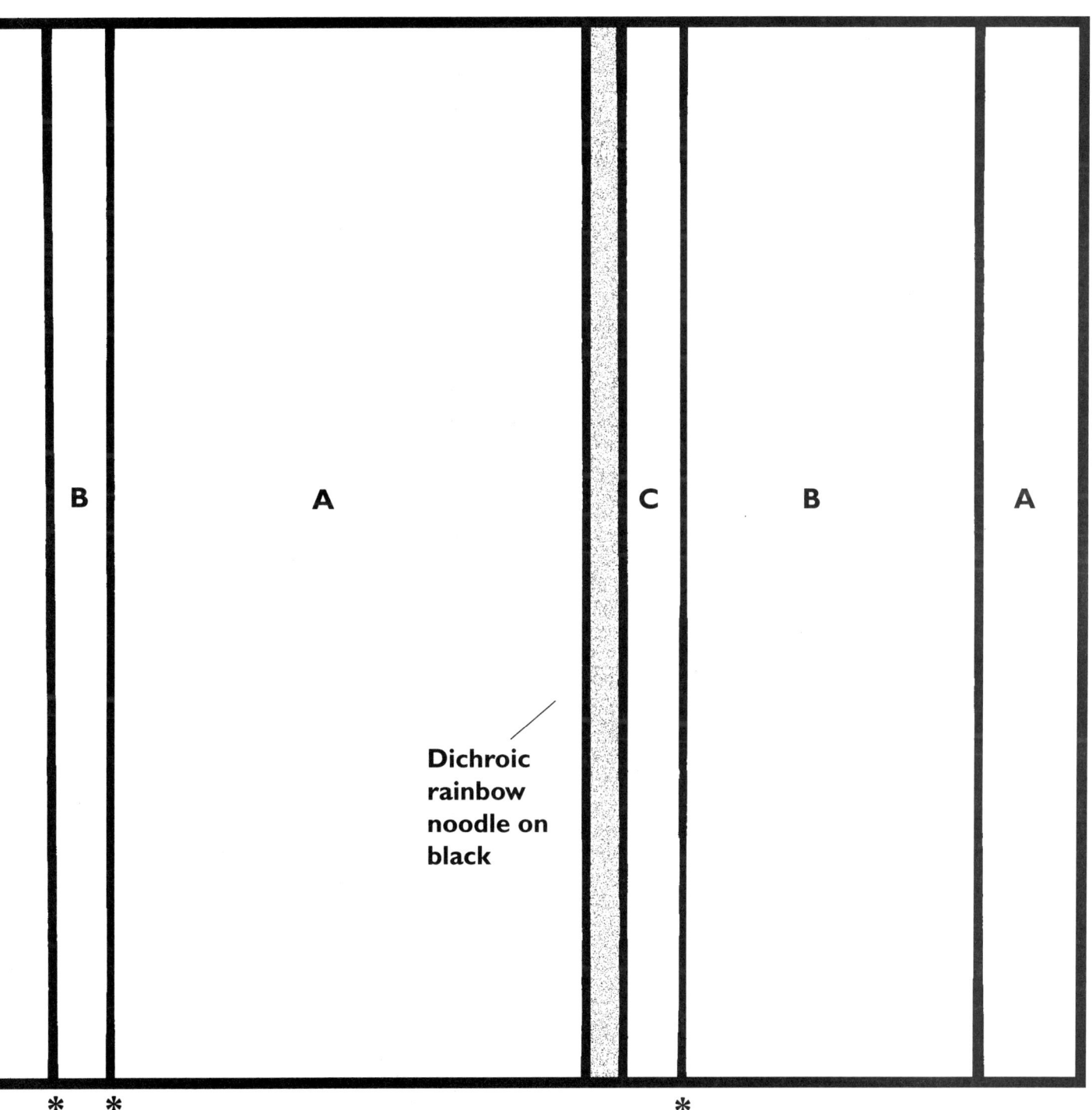

Use outer perimeter as pattern for the lens base.

✼ = **Yellow stringer placement**

Mood Lamp Base

The base is constructed by fusing together three layers of glass:

Layer 1 is cut to the overall size of the lamp base.
Layer 2 is cut in sections to allow for the "groove" into which the lamp lens is adhered.
Layer 3 is three pieces of glass positioned on the front rim of the base. This third layer elevates the rim slightly, allowing for a good bond when gluing the lens to the base.

Detailed instructions for assembling the base can be found on page 19.

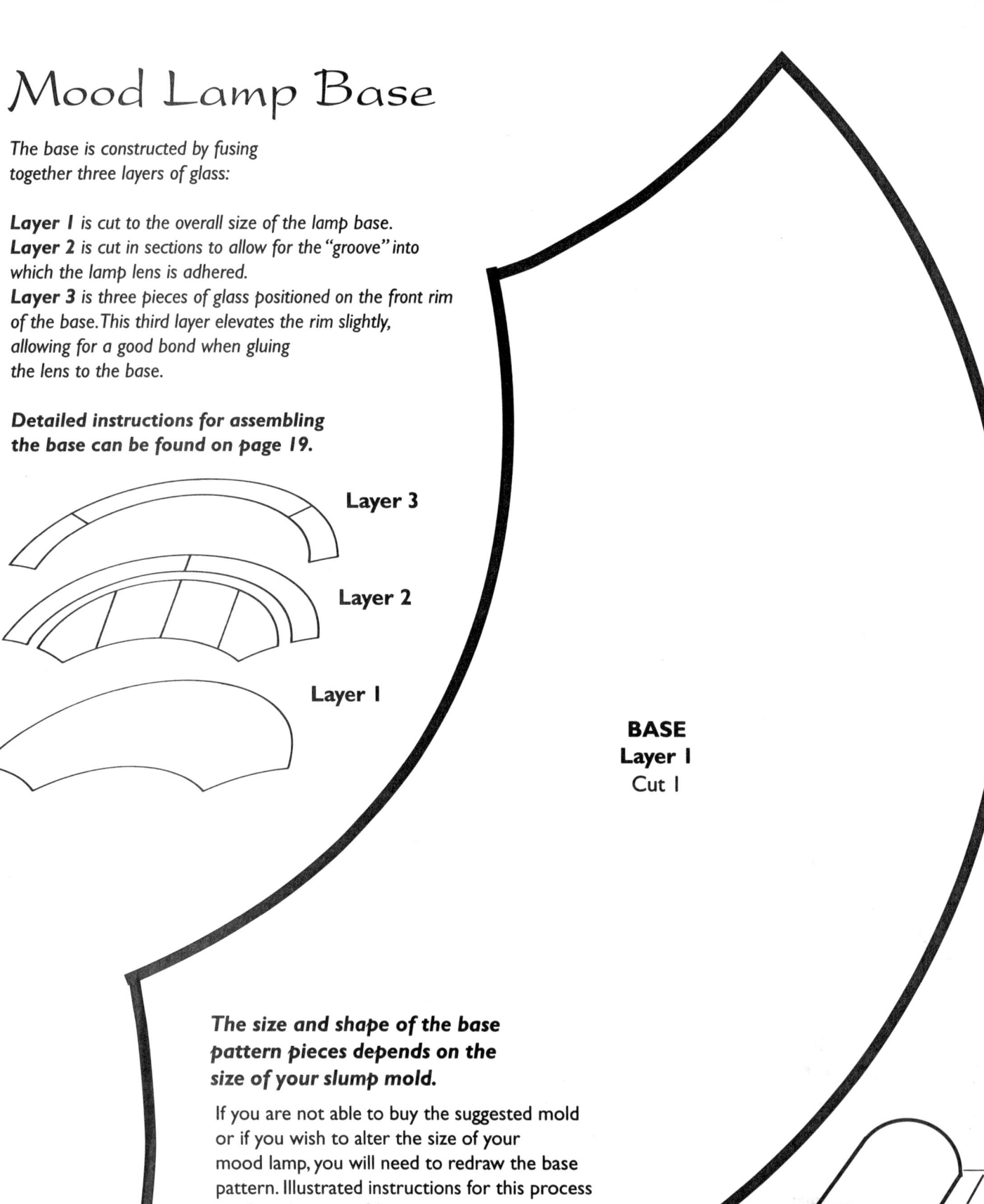

**BASE
Layer 1
Cut 1**

The size and shape of the base pattern pieces depends on the size of your slump mold.

If you are not able to buy the suggested mold or if you wish to alter the size of your mood lamp, you will need to redraw the base pattern. Illustrated instructions for this process are found on page 21.

Approximate dimensions for the Delphi Glass Round Wall Sconce Mold #4270 and Future Forms Round Sconce Mold WC 40

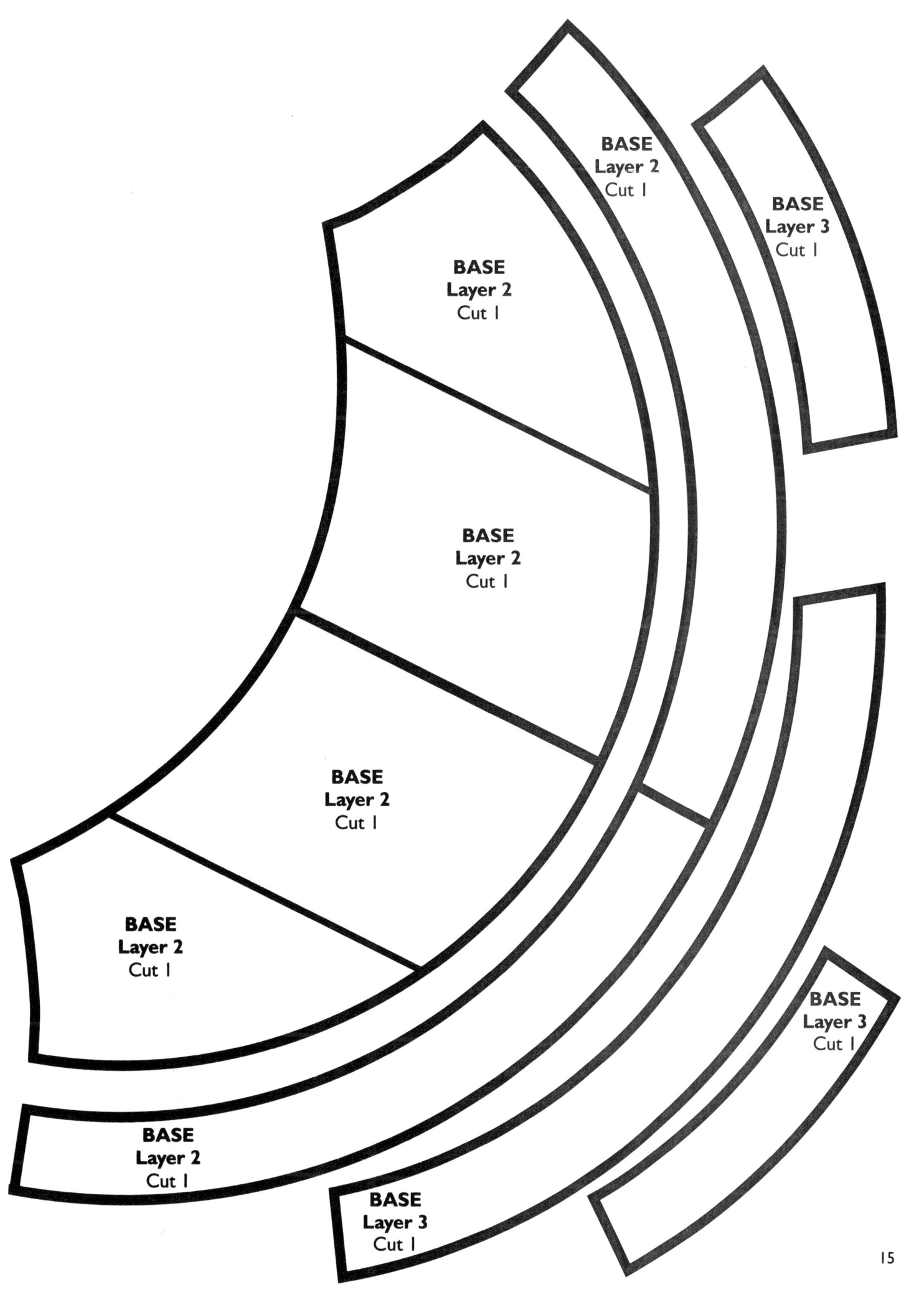

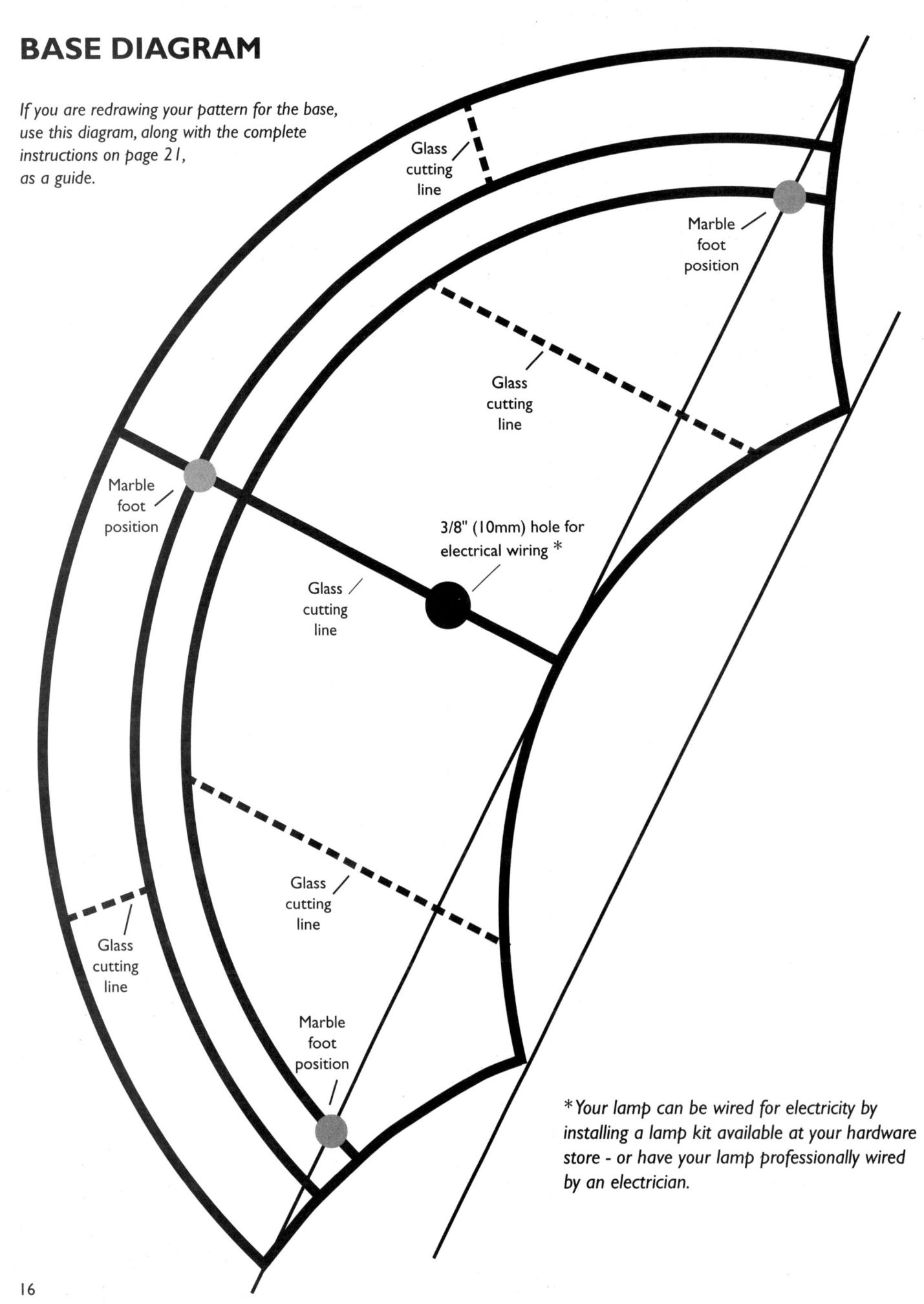

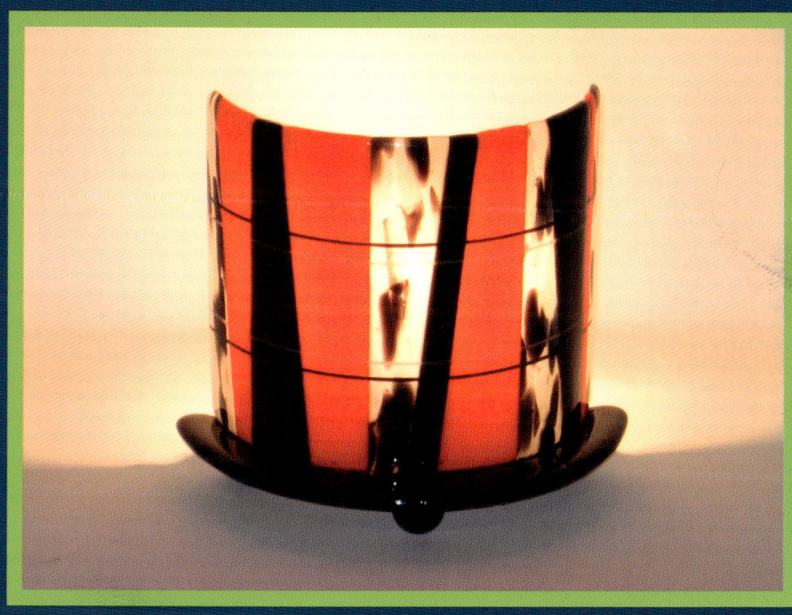

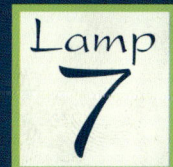

Lamp 7
Africa
Pages 24 & 25

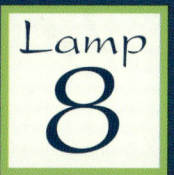

Lamp 8
Harvest
Pages 26 & 27

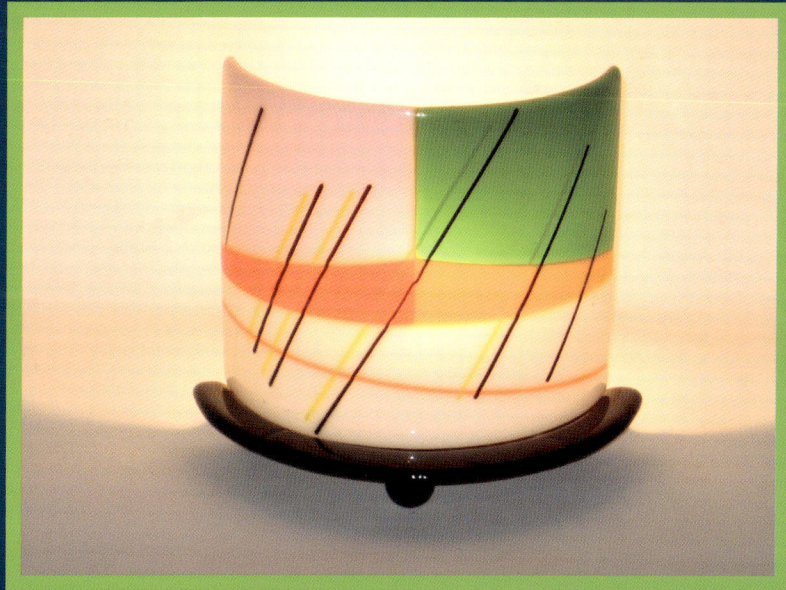

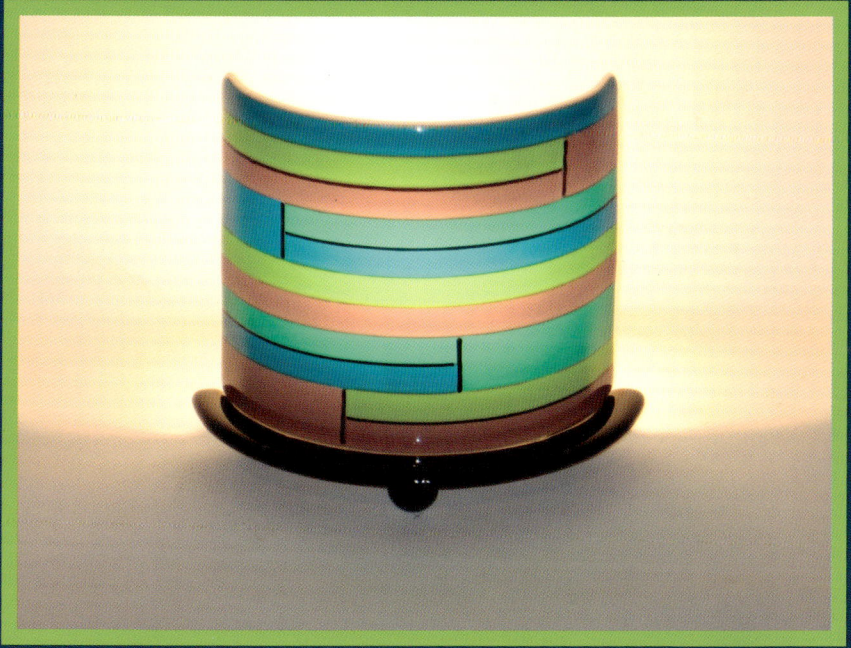

Lamp 9
Lime Slice
Pages 28 & 29

Creating the Mood Lamp Lens . . .

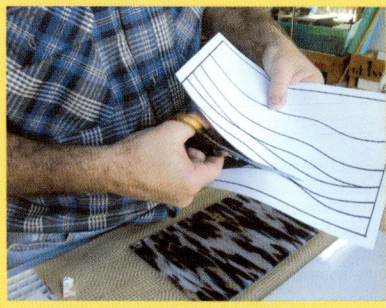 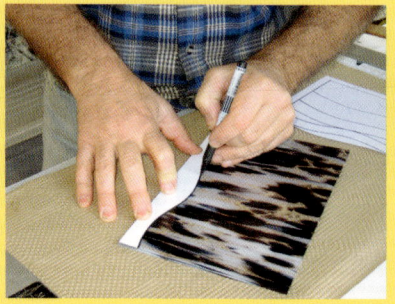 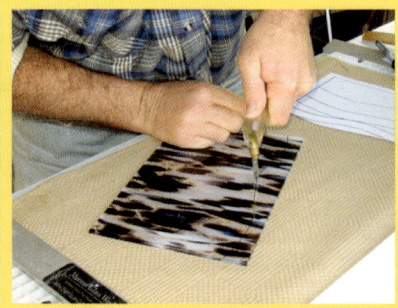

Photocopy or trace 2 copies of selected design onto card stock. Cut around perimeter of one for pattern for lens base. Cut out pattern pieces of other copy to make pattern templates.

Use the pattern templates to trace onto your chosen glass.

Cut the glass for the lens base and the glass for the design layer.

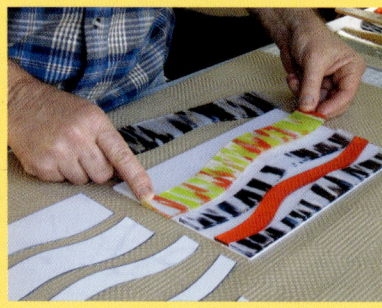 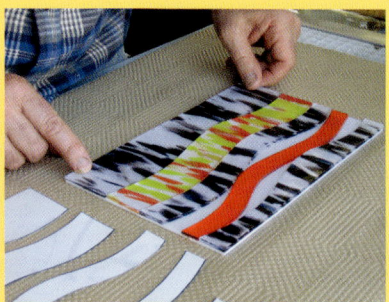 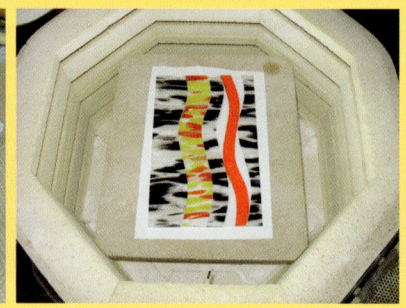

Continue laying out the cut glass pieces onto the lens base until you are satisfied with the design. Be sure the design layer fits accurately within the confines of the base.

The bottom of the lamp lens must be perfectly straight to correctly adhere the lens into the groove in the lamp base.

Fuse the lens according to glass manufacturer's firing schedules. Keep in mind that all kilns are different and some experimentation may be needed.

Slumping the Lens . . .

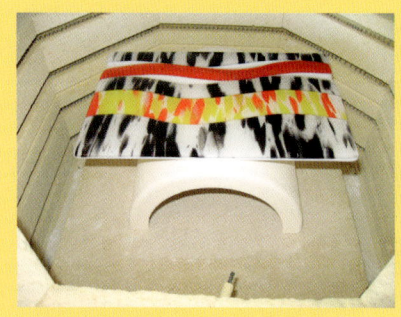 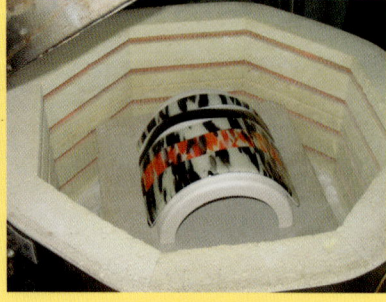 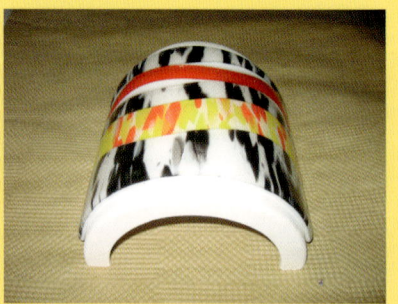

Place mold in kiln. Lay kiln paper over mold. Position lens in center and parallel to edge of mold. (If lens is positioned out of square, the bottom edge will not sit flat, making it difficult to achieve a uniform join when adhering it to base.)

Fire to slump temperature. Don't go too hot or glass will stretch and distort making it impossible to fix to the base. The slump temperature in my kiln is 150 degrees F below the fuse temperature but all kilns are different so fire accordingly.

Your lens is finished and ready to be attached to the base. Clean it thoroughly and set it aside until you have built your base.

Fusing the Mood Lamp Base . . .

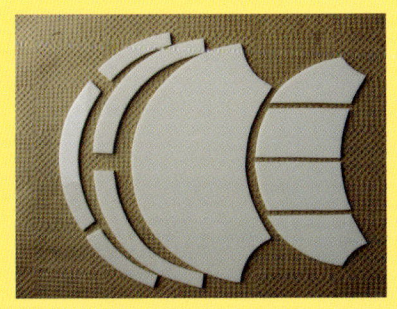

1. Cut all glass for the base. If your slump mold is the same or similar in size to the mold used in this book, it is a simple matter of using the pattern supplied on pages 14 to 16. To check if your lamp lens fits the supplied pattern, place your lens on top of the pattern and compare the curve and adjust the groove line if needed, as long as you allow the necessary 3/8" gap for the lens to be adhered to the base.

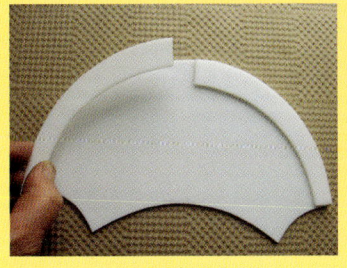 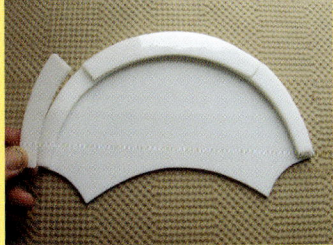 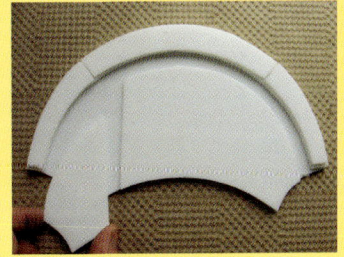 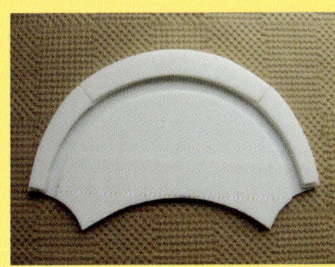

Layer the first row of edge glass onto the bottom layer.

Layer the second row of edge glass onto the bottom layer.

Layer the four sections of glass onto bottom layer.

Assembled base ready for fusing.

When the base is assembled on the kiln shelf, fire to dimensional fuse temperature. This is very important as the base must have a definite groove in which to glue the lens. A full fuse temperature will not result in this necessary groove.

Assembling the Mood Lamp . . .

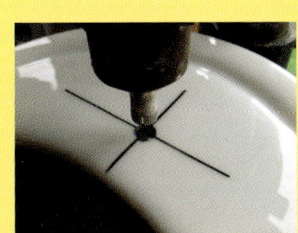 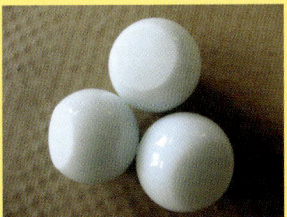 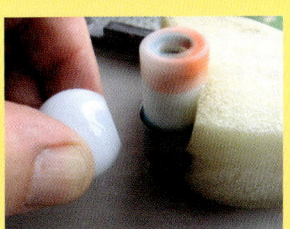 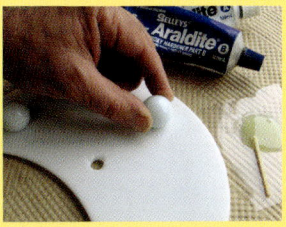

Drill hole for electrical fitting with a glass grinder and 1/4" glass bit - or a drill press and 3/8" hollow core diamond drill bit.

Three 1" diameter glass marbles are used for the feet. (A suitable alternative would be wooden balls painted the color of the base.)

Use a glass grinder to grind a flat spot appr. 3/8" diameter onto each glass marble.

Glue each marble onto the underside of the base using a two part epoxy glue. (See diagram on page 16.)

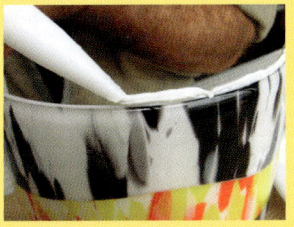 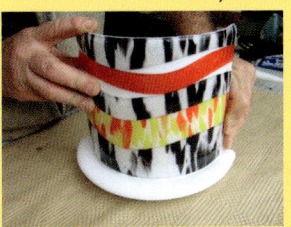 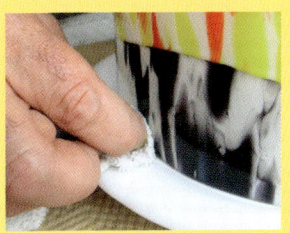 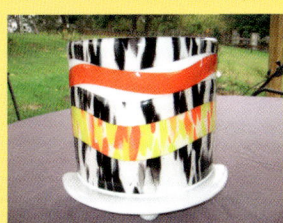

Clean base and lens. Apply a bead of adhesive sealant 1/8" thick to bottom edge of lens.

Position the bottom edge of lens into the groove in the base and press down firmly.

Clean off excess adhesive using solvent recommended by manufacturer. Allow adhesive to cure for recommended time.

And now, your lamp is ready to be wired and enjoyed!

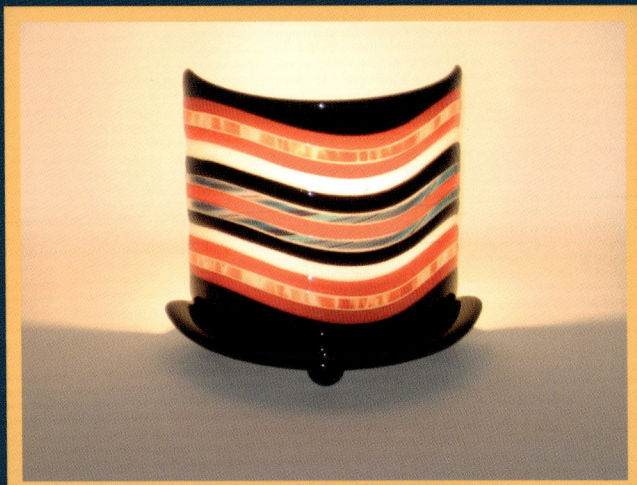

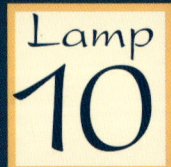

Lamp 10
Rainbow Serpent
Pages 30 & 31

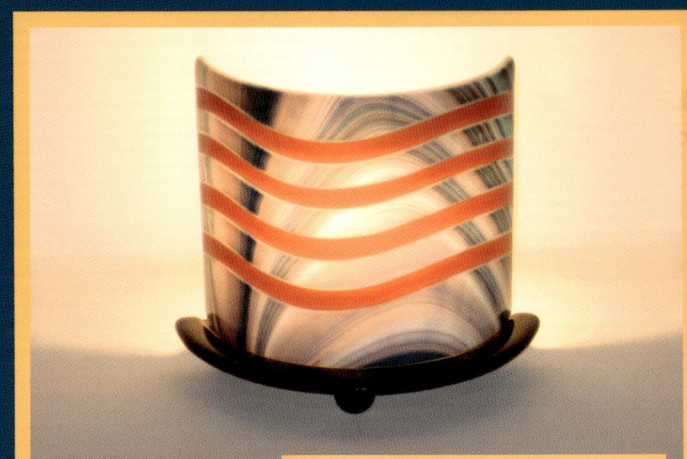

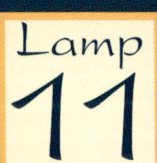

Lamp 11
Peaceful Flow
Pages 32 & 33

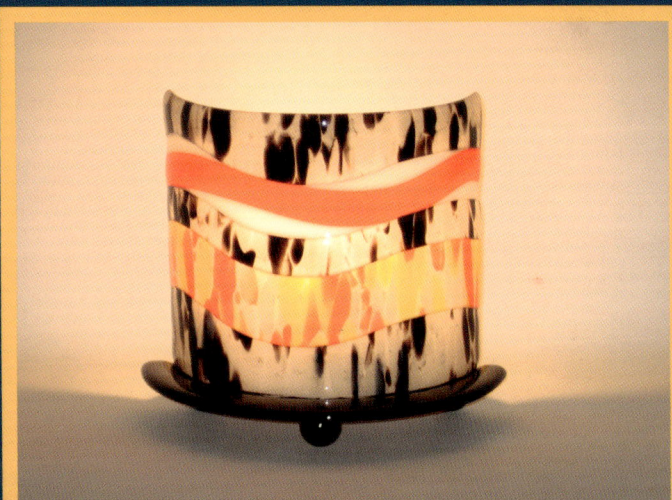

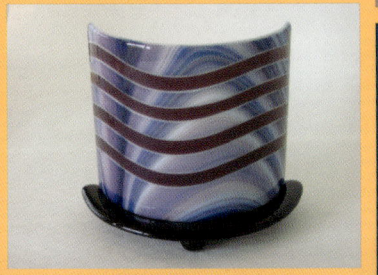

Peaceful Flow
Color variation

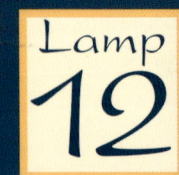

Lamp 12
Sunset
Pages 34 & 35

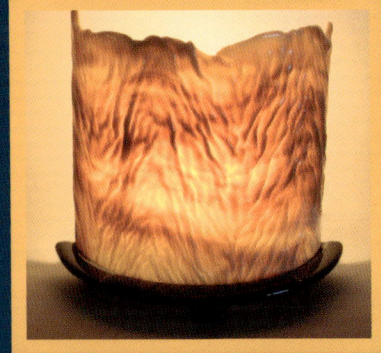 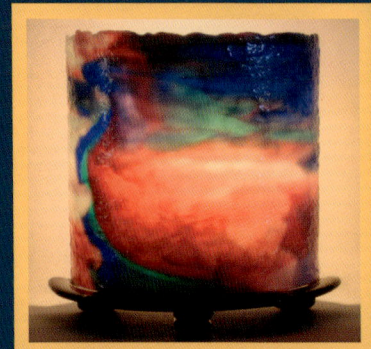 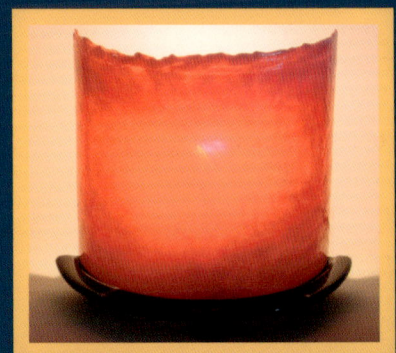

These stunning Mood Lamps are created by slumping a single sheet of art glass over the mold. Note that the rolled edges have been left intact for added interest.

Resizing the Base Pattern

After buying your mold, fuse and slump your lamp lens. Place your lens on top of the pattern and compare the curve. Adjust the groove line as needed. Be sure to allow the necessary 3/8 inch gap for the lens to be adhered to the base. If it fits, you're all set! If not, adjust your base pattern like this:

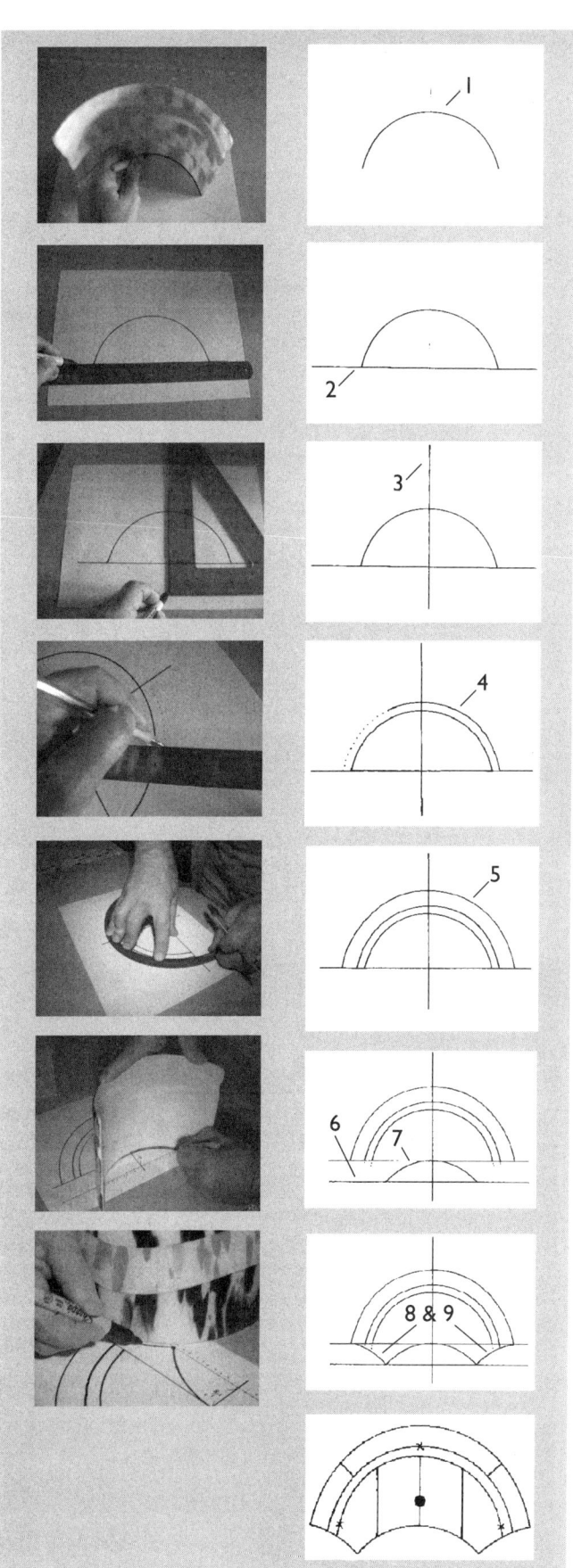

Line 1 Place your lamp lens on a piece of paper. Using a marker, trace along the inner edge of the lens. Begin on one corner and follow the full length of the lens or curve.

Line 2 Draw a line connecting the two outer corners of the curve, and extend to the outer edges of the paper.

Line 3 Now measure the length of Line 2 and determine the center point of that line. Place a triangle on that center mark and draw a line at 90 degrees from that point (as shown in the diagram) the full width of your piece of paper.

Line 4 Place a ruler on the center point of Line 3, pivot from the center measuring and extending 3/8" out from Line 1, following the curve and marking the measurement point with dots as you go. When complete, join up the dots.

Line 5 This is the same procedure as drawing Line 4, but this time extend the measurement 1 1/8". Measure, mark the dots and then connect them to form a line. You might find it helpful to use a flexible curve to draw the line.

Line 6 Draw a line 1 1/8" below and parallel to Line 1.
Line 7 Using the inside curve of your lamp lens, position the lens centering it as shown in the diagram between Line 2 and Line 6. Trace the line with a marking pen.

Lines 8 and 9 Use your lamp lens to draw a connecting curve between the bottom points of Line 7 and the end points of Line 5.

Glass Cutting Lines and Electrical Wiring Hole Draw in the glass cutting lines that are shown on the full-size diagram on page 16.

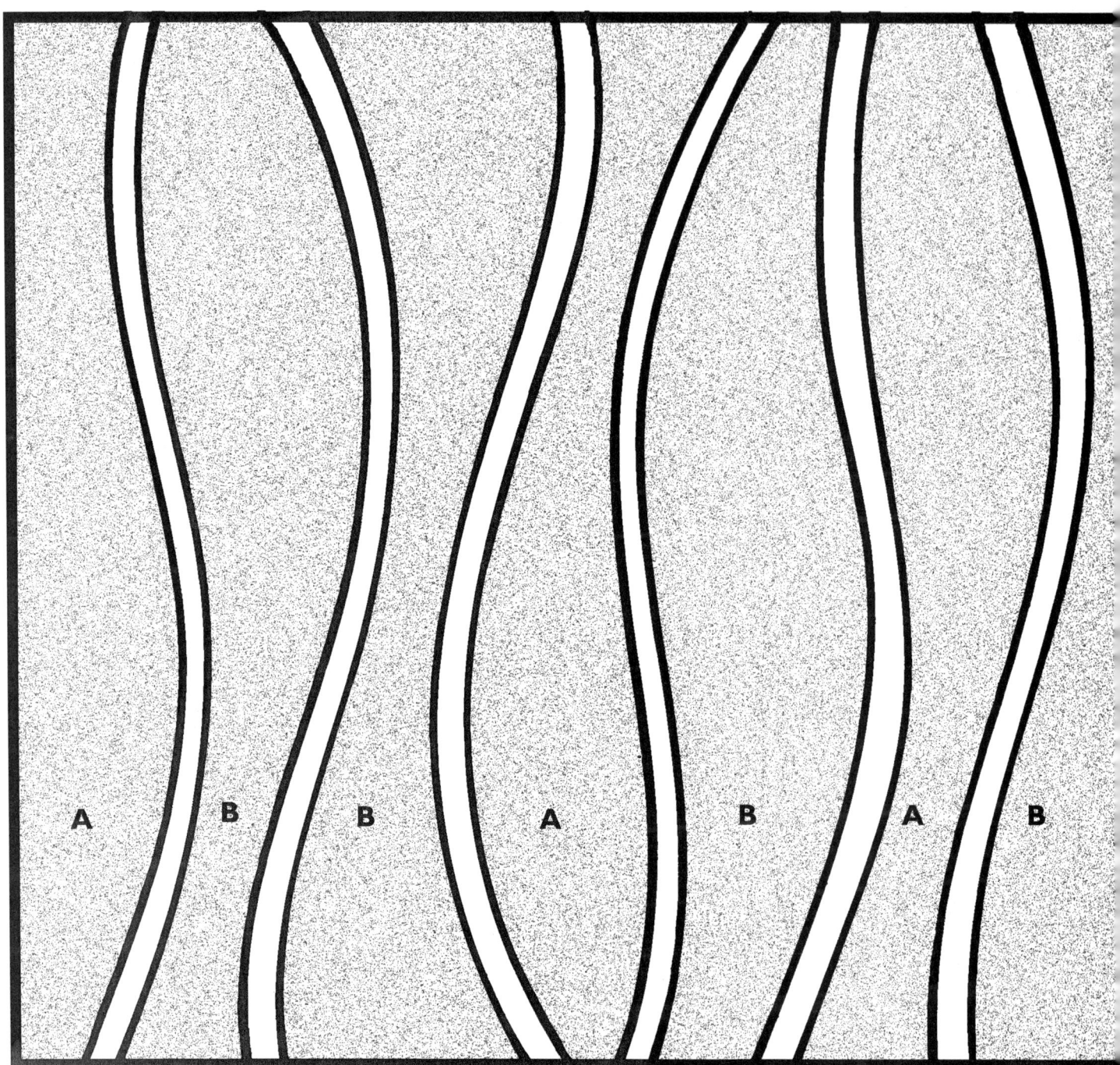

Use outer perimeter as pattern for the lens base.

// = **Base Layer**

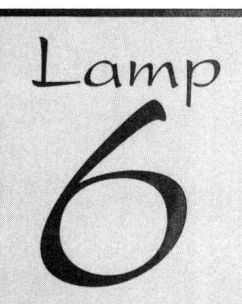

Purple Haze — Lamp 6

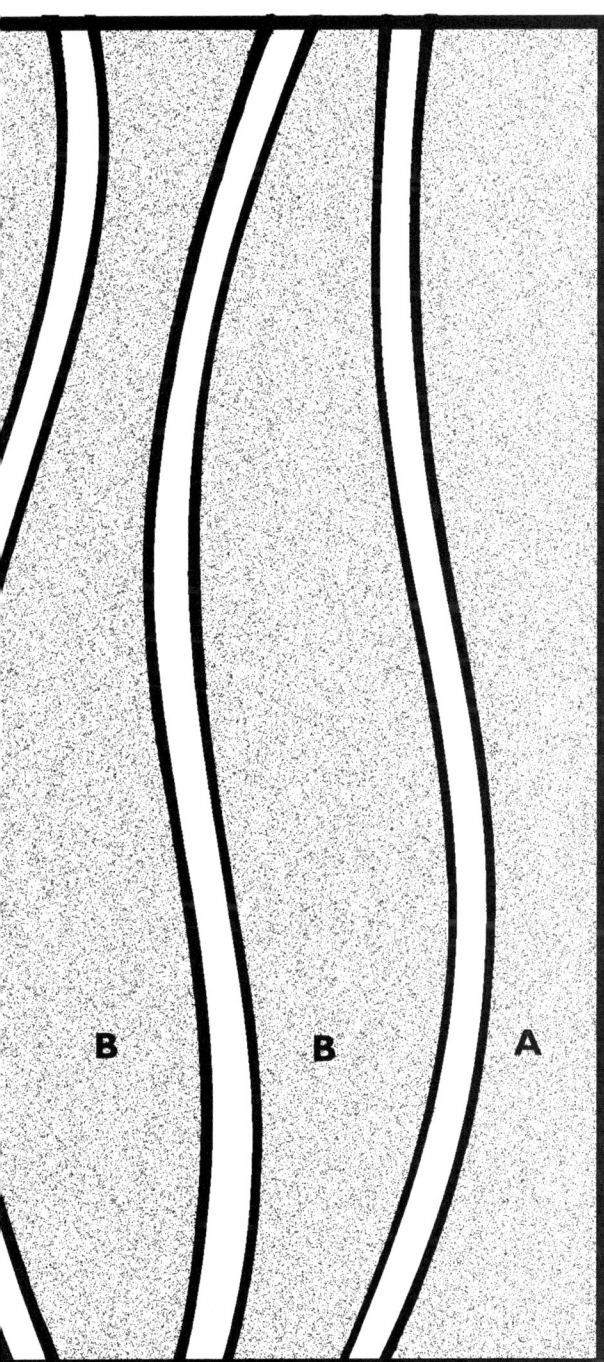

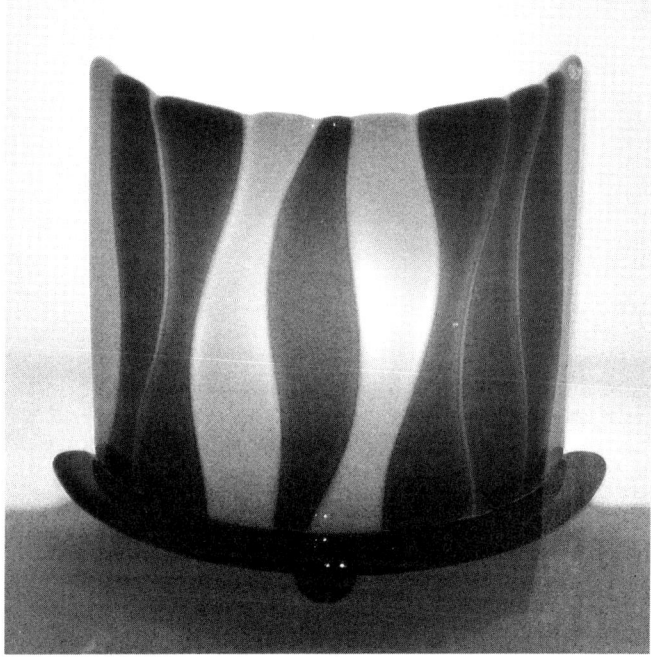

Lamp Base	Spectrum System 96 - Black Opal 1009SF
Lens Base	Spectrum System 96 - White Opal - 200SF
Top Design Layer	Spectrum System 96 - **A** ... Grape Transparent 543-2SF
	B ... Cotton Candy Pink Opal 290-72SF

• Cut one lens base the size of pattern above.
• Cut one of each top design layer, marked "**A & B**". Place these pieces on top of lens base following indications on pattern.
• See the detailed instructions on pages 18 and 19 for fabricating the lens and base.

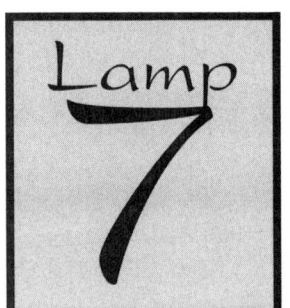

Lamp 7 Africa

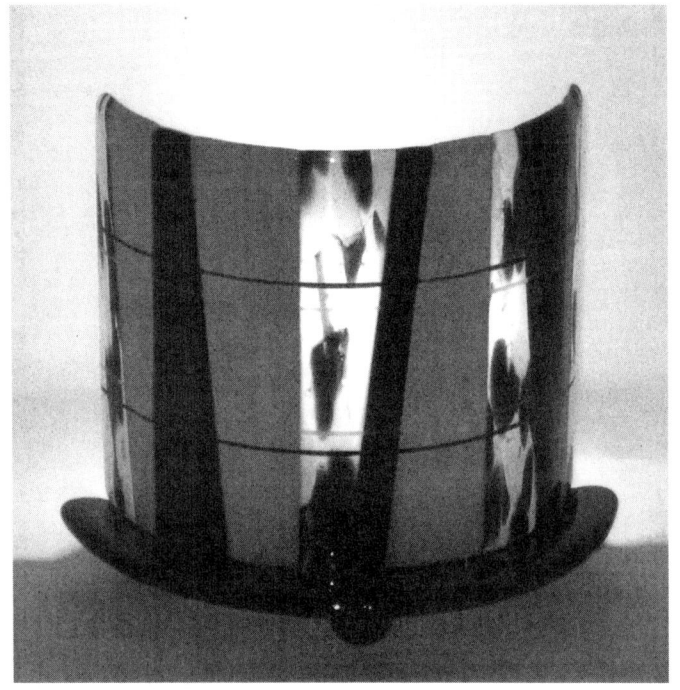

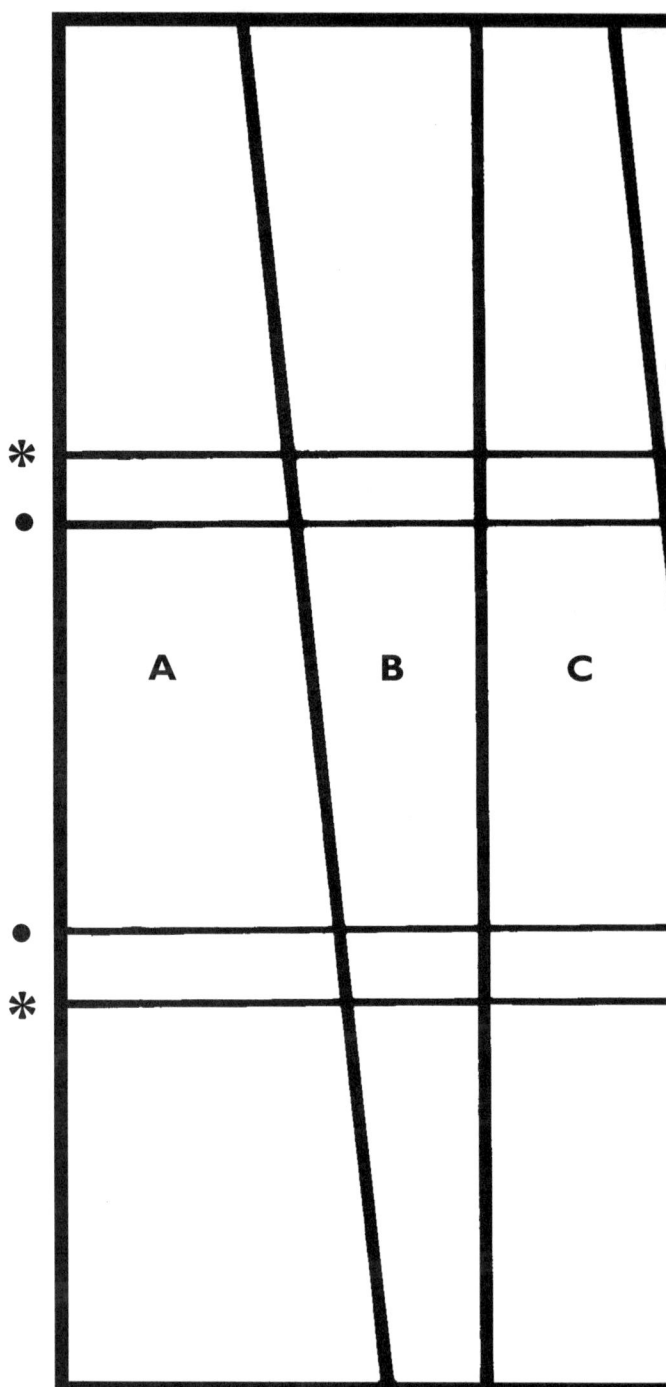

A	B	C

Lamp Base   Spectrum System 96 - Black Opal   1009SF
Lens Base   Spectrum System 96 - White Opal - 200SF
Top Design Layer   Spectrum System 96 - **A** ... Spirit 4001SF Murano
                    Uroboros System 96 - **B** ... Red Opal 60-2702-96
                    Spectrum System 96 - **C** ... Black Opal 1009SF
                    White Stringer
                    Black Stringer

• Cut one lens base the size of pattern above.
• Cut one of each top design layer, marked "**A**, **B** & **C**". Place these pieces on top of lens base following indications on pattern.
• Position stringer as indicated.
• See the detailed instructions on pages 18 and 19 for fabricating the lens and base.

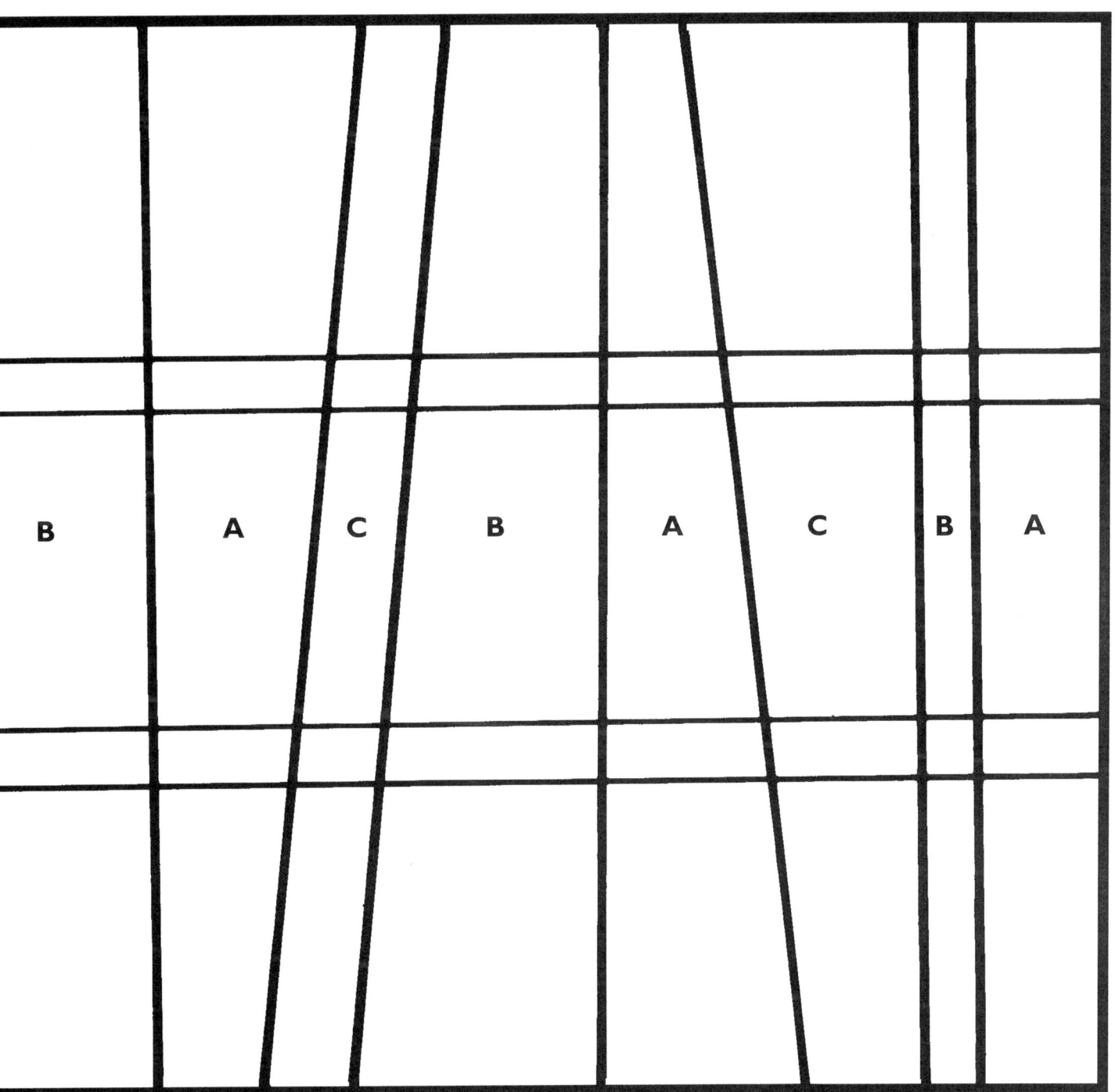

Use outer perimeter as pattern for the lens base.

✻ = **Black stringer placement**
● = **White stringer placement**

Note: Stringer is positioned on top of glass strips.

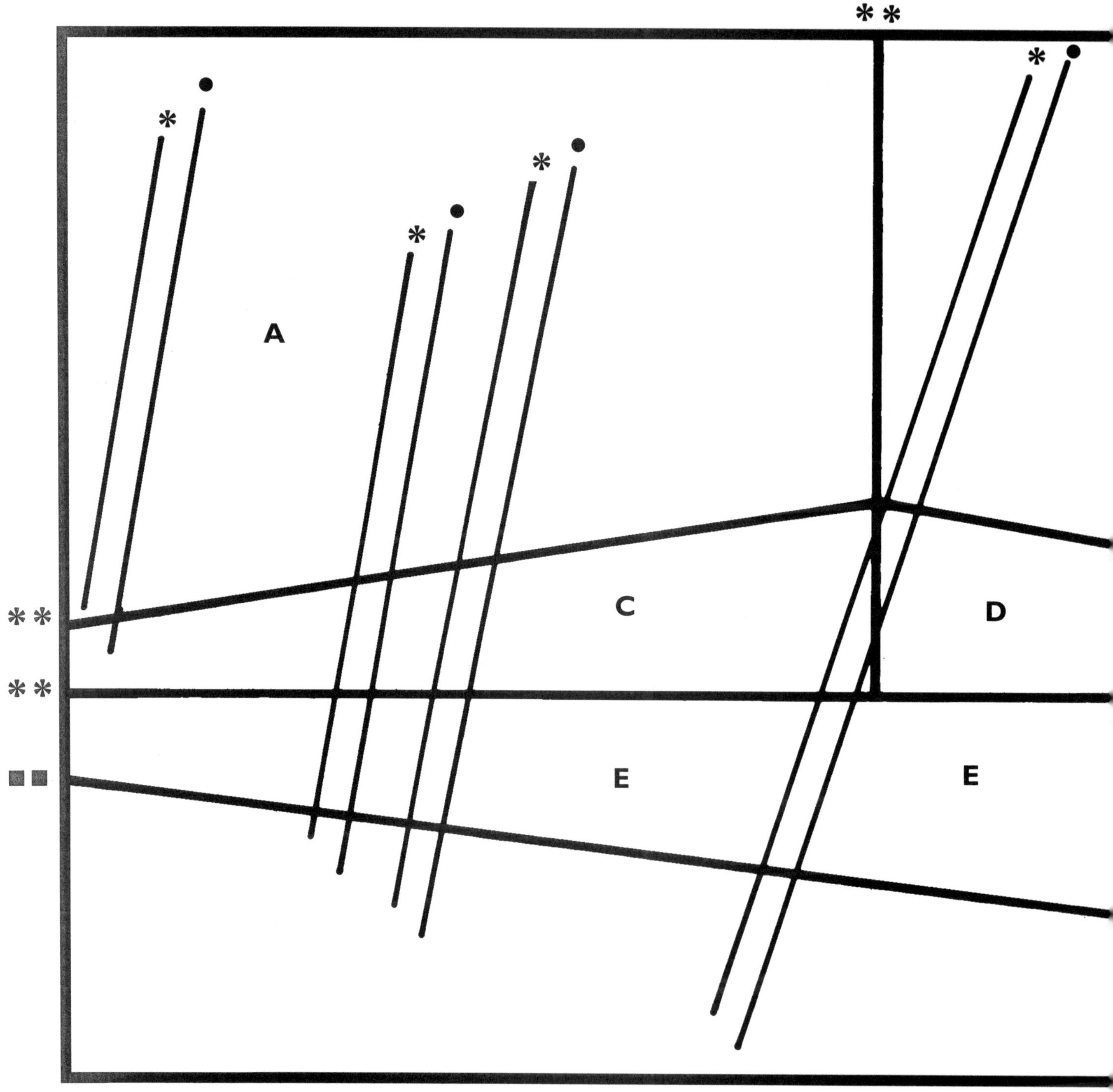

Use outer perimeter as pattern for the lens base.

* = Yellow stringer placement

● = Black stringer placement

* * = Yellow stringer - 2 layers stacked between cut glass pieces

■ ■ = Orange stringer - 2 layers stacked between cut glass pieces

Harvest Lamp 8

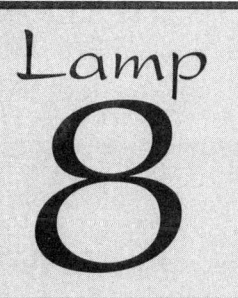

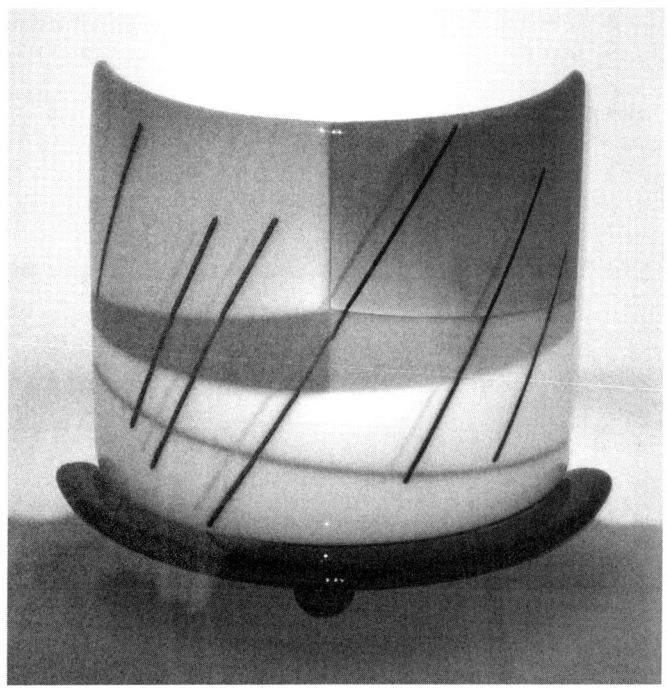

Lamp Base	Spectrum System 96 - Black Opal 1009SF
Lens Base	Spectrum System 96 - White Opal 200SF
Top Design Layer	Spectrum System 96 - **A** ... Cotton Candy Pink Opal 290-72SF
	Spectrum System 96 - **B** ... Moss Green Trans 526-2SF
	Uroboros System 96 - **C** ... Orange Opal 60-2702-96
	Spectrum System 96 - **D** .. Yellow Opal 260-72SF
	Spectrum System 96 - **E** ... White Opal 200SF
	Yellow Stringer, Black Stringer, Orange Stringer

- Cut one lens base the size of pattern above.
- Cut one of each top design layer, marked "**A**, **B**, **C**, **D** & **E**". Place these pieces on top of lens base according to pattern. In between each piece, place two pieces of orange or yellow stringer sitting on top of each other as indicated on pattern.
- Position yellow and black stringer as indicated.
- See the detailed instructions on pages 18 and 19 for fabricating the lens and base.

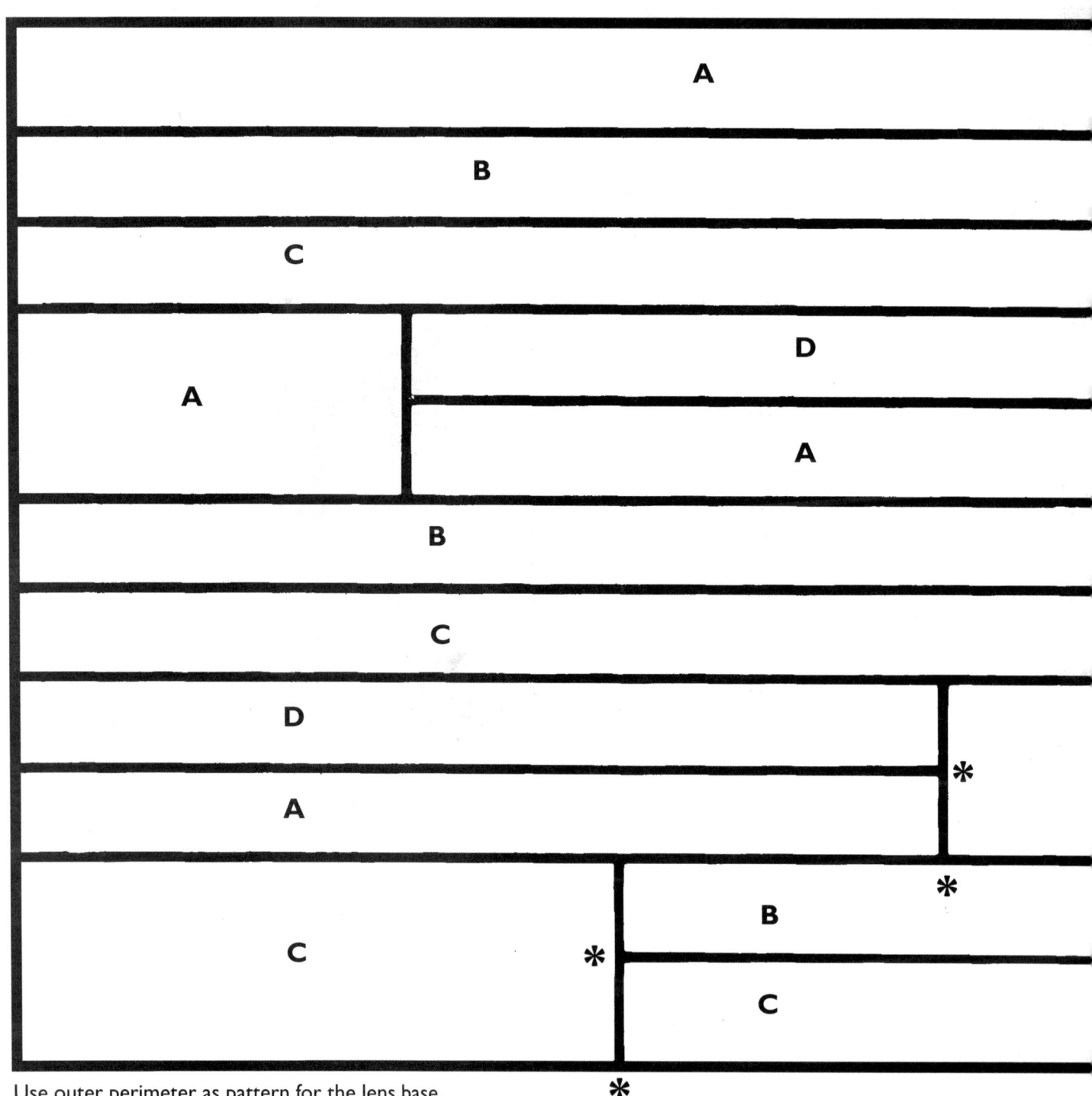

Use outer perimeter as pattern for the lens base.

✽ = Black stringer placement

Note: Stringer is positioned on top of of design at designated cut lines.

Lamp 9

Lime Slice

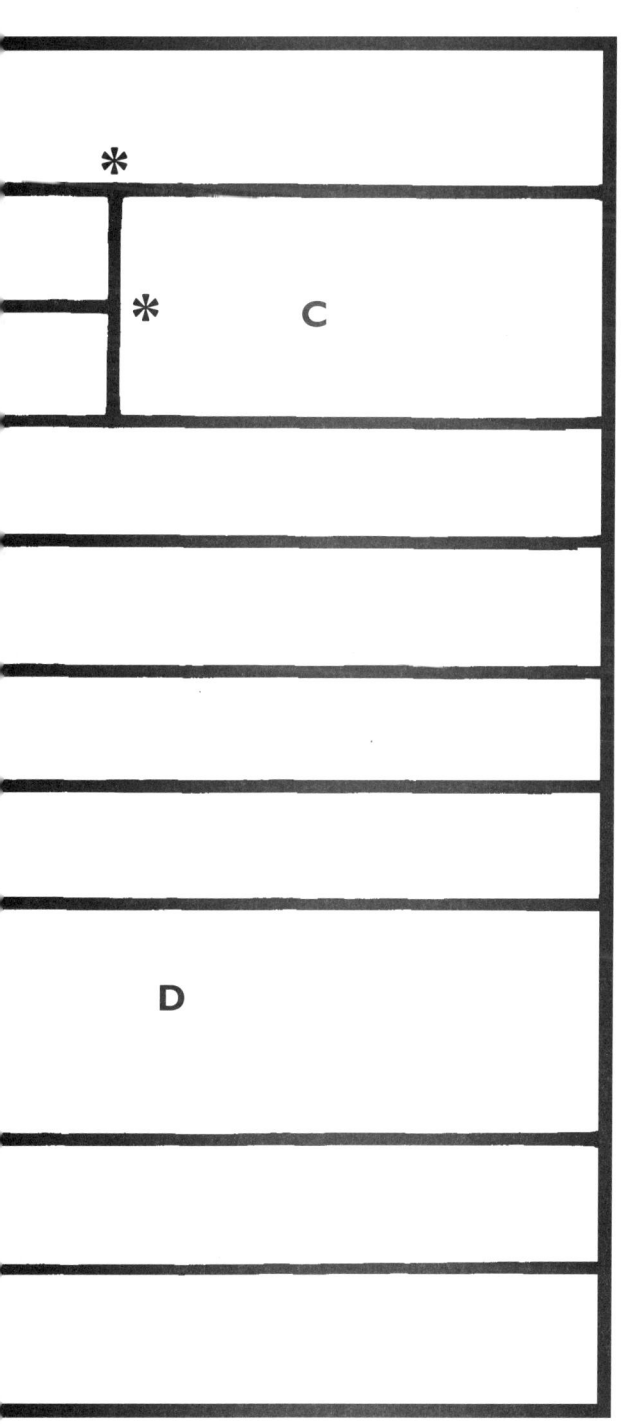

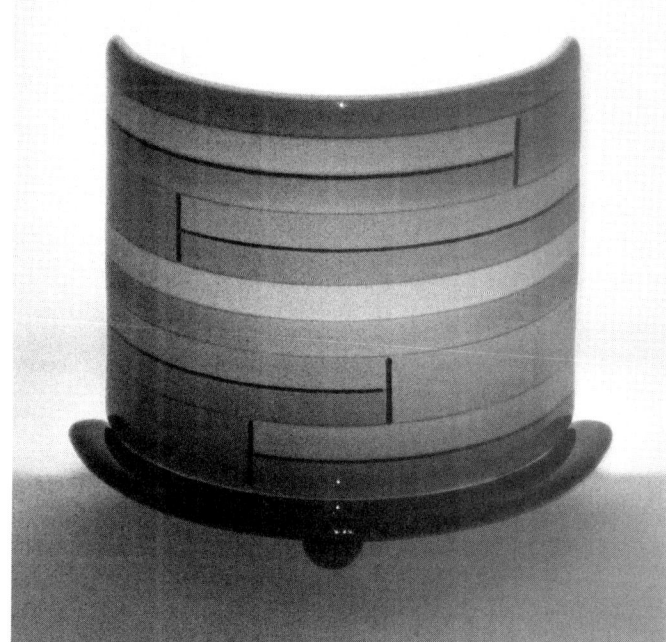

Lamp Base	Spectrum System 96 - Black Opal 1009SF
Lens Base	Spectrum System 96 - White Opal 200SF
Top Design Layer	Spectrum System 96 - **A** ... Deep Aqua Transparent 533-3SF
	Spectrum System 96 - **B** ... Moss Green Transparent 526-2SF
	Spectrum System 96 - **C** ... Grape Transparent 543-2SF
	Spectrum System 96 - **D** ... Teal Transparent 523-2SF
	Black Stringer

- Cut one lens base the size of pattern above.
- Cut one of each top design layer, marked "**A**, **B**, **C** & **D**". Place these pieces on top of lens base following indications on pattern.
- Position stringer as indicated.
- See the detailed instructions on pages 18 and 19 for fabricating the lens and base.

Lamp 10 — Rainbow Serpent

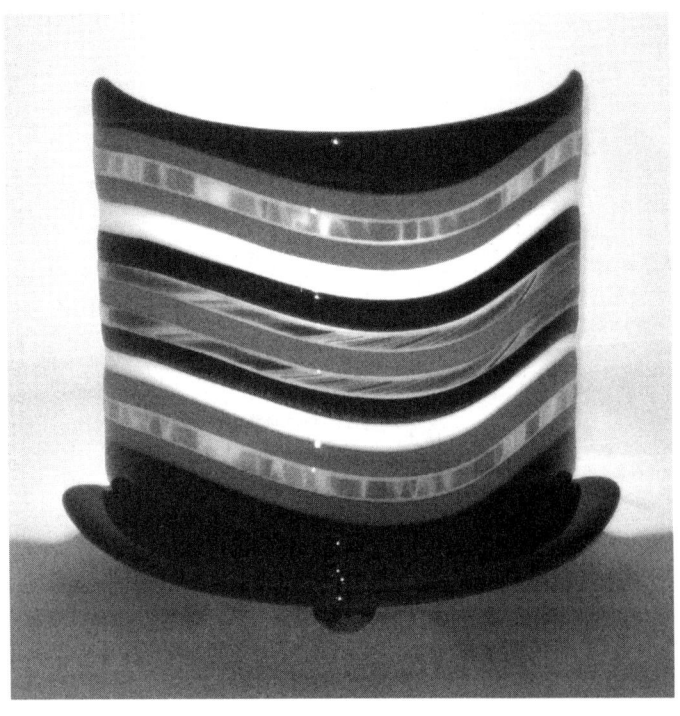

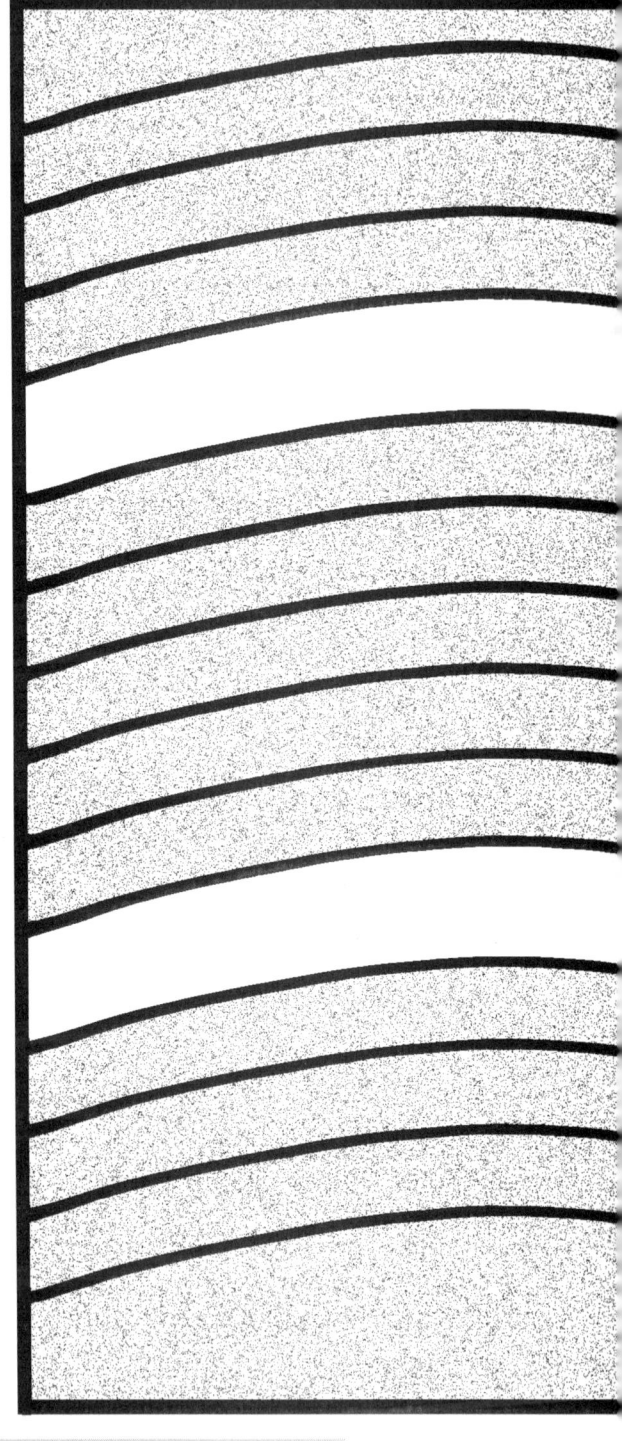

Lamp Base	Spectrum System 96 -	Black Opal 1009SF
Lens Base	Spectrum System 96 -	White Opal 200SF
Top Design Layer	Spectrum System 96 -	**A** ...Black Opal 1009SF
		B ... Cherry Red Transparent 151SF
		C ... Spirit 6115-72SF Sedona
		D ... Opal Art OA/634-52SF

- Cut one lens base the size of pattern above.
- Cut one of each top design layer, marked "**A, B, C & D**". Place these pieces on top of lens base following indications on pattern.
- See the detailed instructions on pages 18 and 19 for fabricating the lens and base.

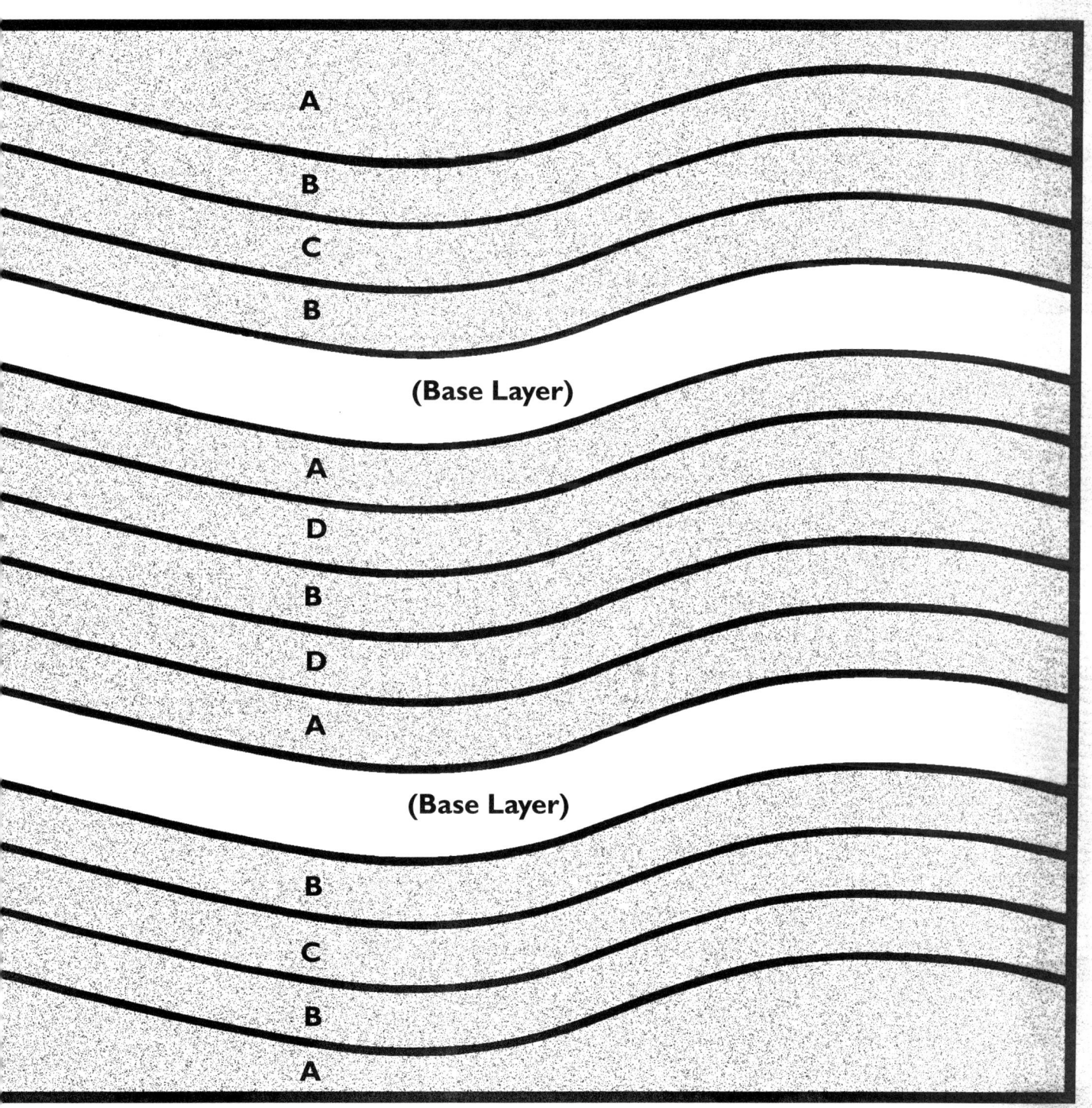

Use outer perimeter as pattern for the lens base.

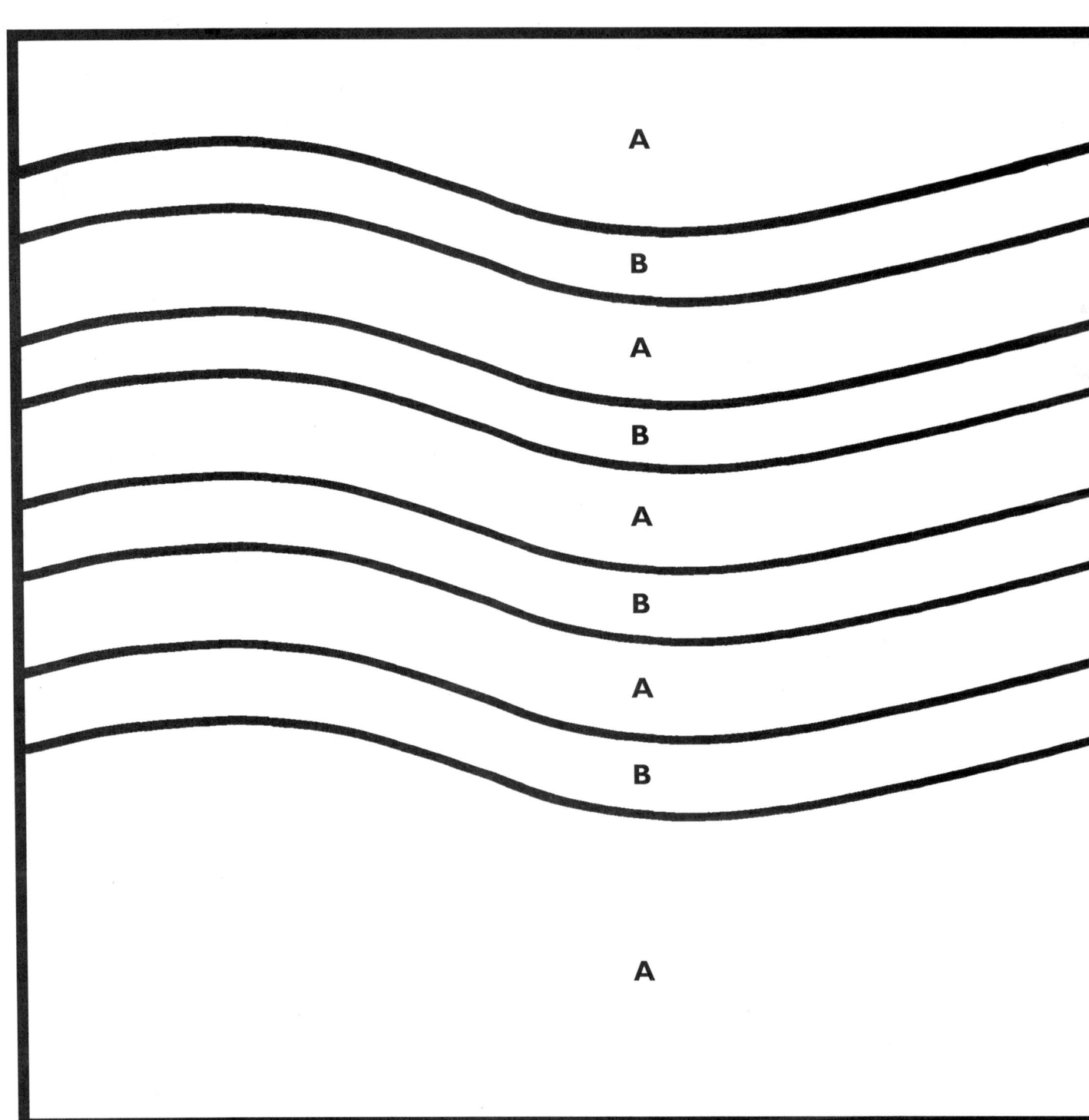

Use outer perimeter as pattern for the lens base.

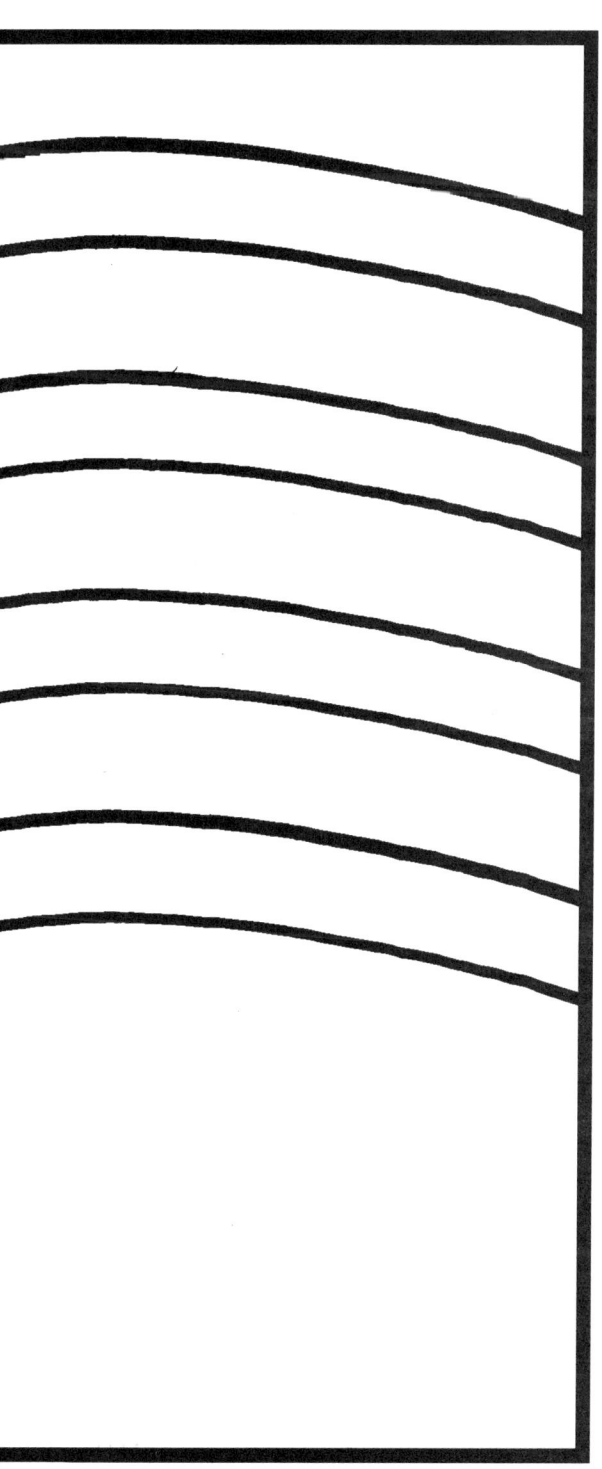

Peaceful Flow

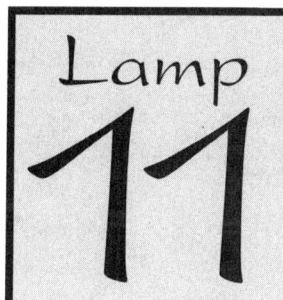

Lamp 11

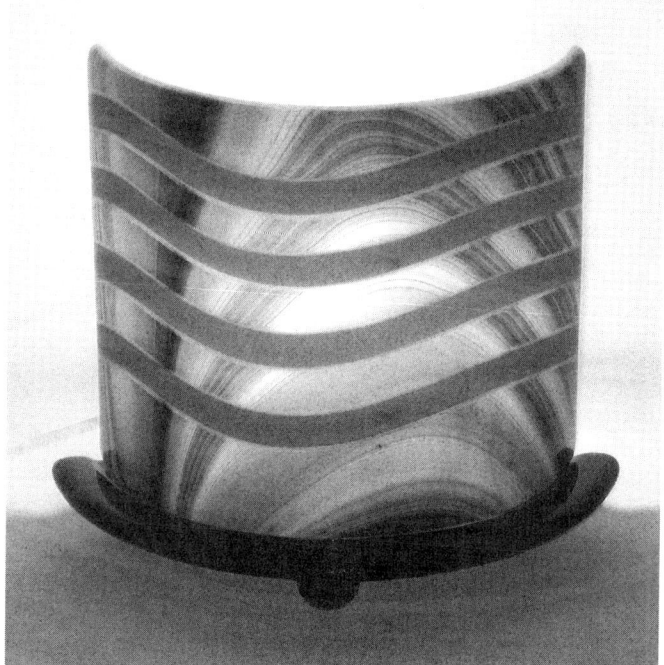

Lamp Base	Spectrum System 96 - Black Opal 1009SF
Lens Base	Spectrum System 96 - White Opal 200SF
Top Design Layer	Spectrum System 96 - **A** ...Opal Art OA/ 634-52SF
	B ... Cherry Red Transparent 151SF

• Cut one lens base the size of pattern above.
• Cut one of each top design layer, marked "**A & B**". Place these pieces on top of lens base following indications on pattern.
• When cutting the Blackberry Opal Art begin with one piece the correct width. Cut one wavy strip, then work your way down in sequence, keeping them in the order of cutting. This allows for the flow of the Opal art lines to flow nicely thoughout your lamp.
• See the detailed instructions on pages 18 and 19 for fabricating the lens and base.

Lamp 12 Sunset

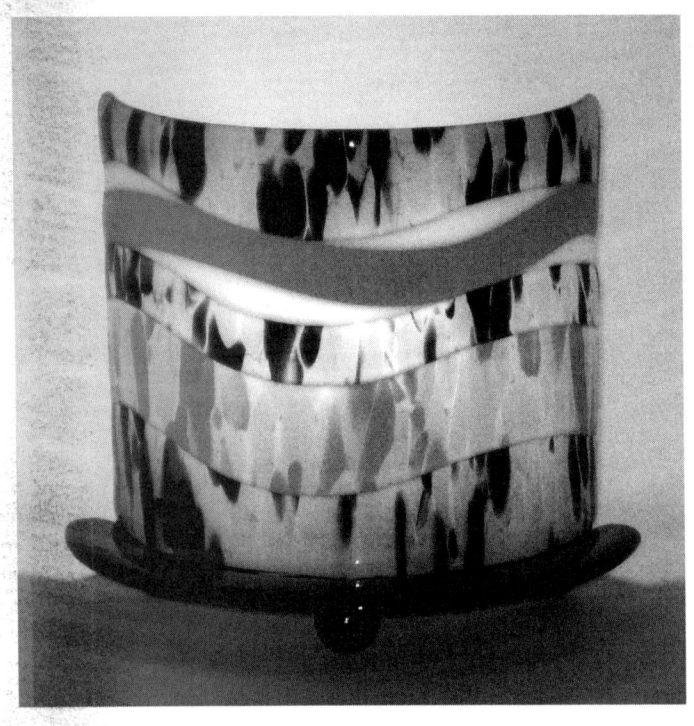

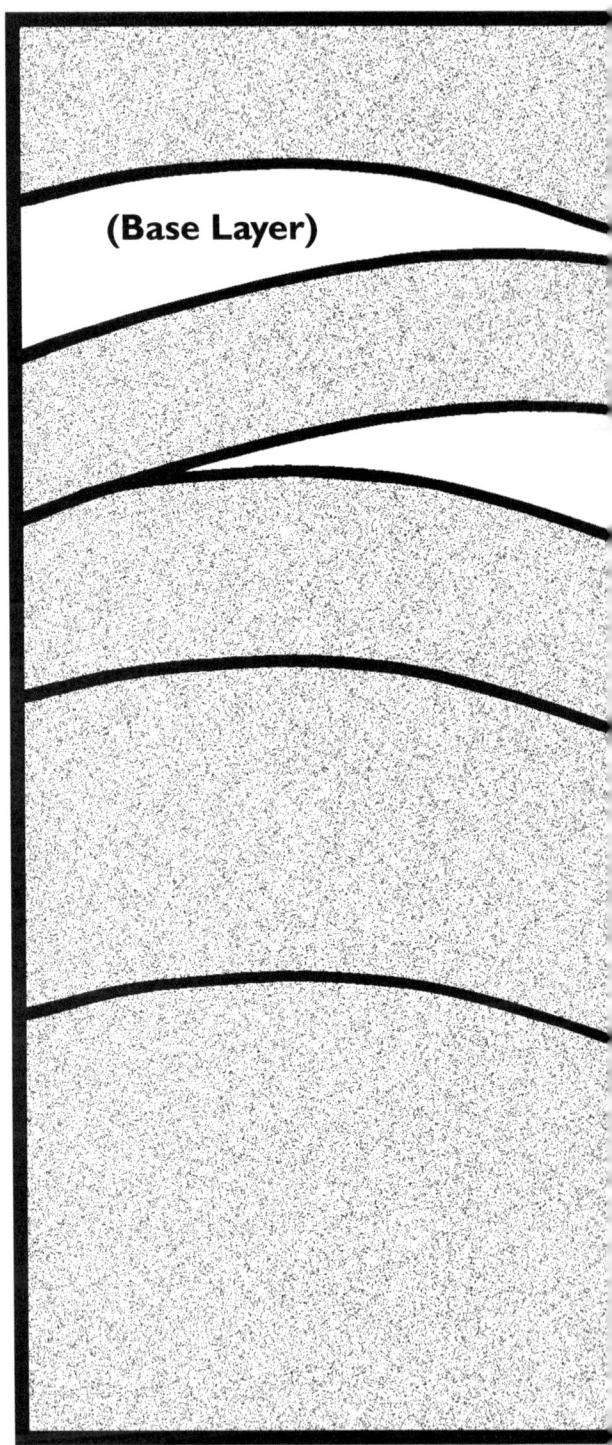

(Base Layer)

Lamp Base	Spectrum System 96 - Black Opal 1009SF
Lens Base	Spectrum System 96 - White Opal 200SF
Top Design Layer	Spectrum System 96 - **A** ... Spirit 4001SF Murano
	Spectrum System 96 - **B** ... Orange Transparent 171SF
	Uroboros System 96 - **C** ... Spirit 4561SF Rio

- Cut one lens base the size of pattern above.
- Cut one of each top design layer, marked "**A, B** & **C**". Place these pieces on top of lens base following indications on pattern.
- See the detailed instructions on pages 18 and 19 for fabricating the lens and base.

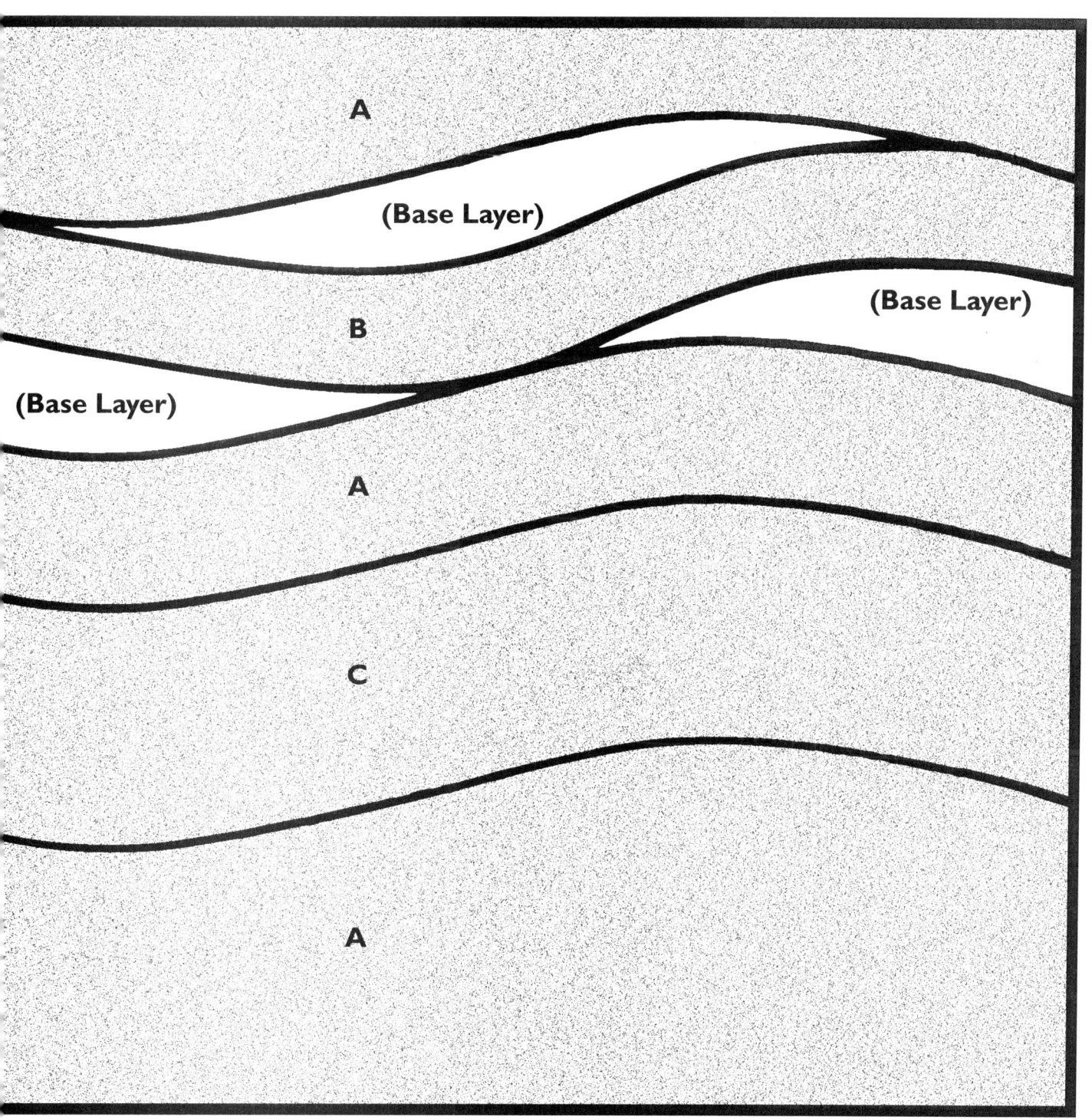

Use outer perimeter as pattern for the lens base.

Lamp 13 — Spring Night

A B A B A B A B A B A B A

Enlarge pattern to 11 ½" wide or as needed for your mold..

Use outer perimeter of enlarged version as pattern for the lens base.

Lamp 14 — Fire Storm

A A A A

Enlarge pattern to 11 ½" wide or as needed for your mold..

Use outer perimeter of enlarged version as pattern for the lens base.

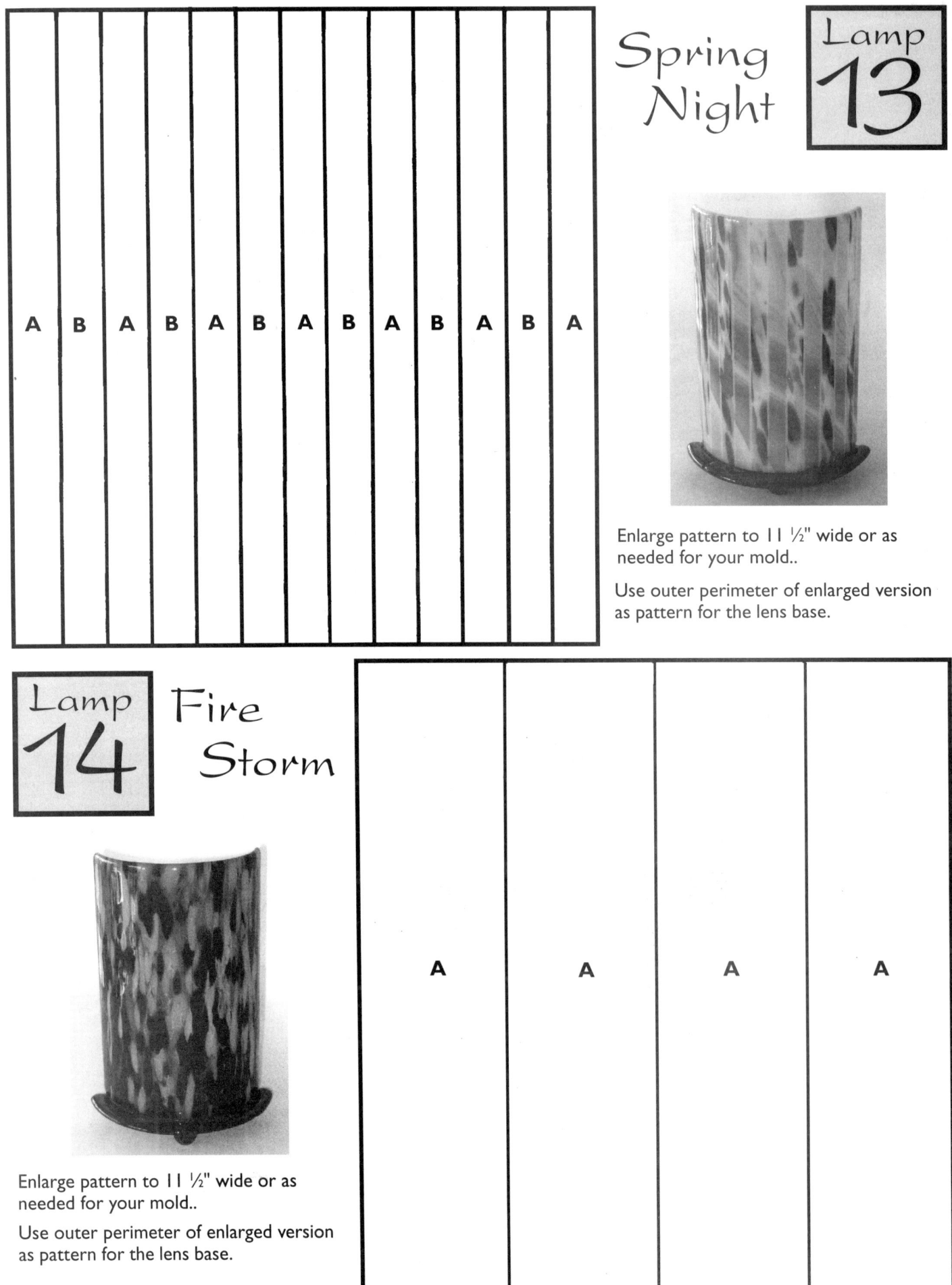